TKINTER, DATA SCIENCE, AND MACHINE LEARNING

VIVIAN SIAHAAN
RISMON HASIHOLAN SIANIPAR

Published: AGUST 2023
Production reference: 4280123
Published by BALIGE Publishing Ltd.
BALIGE, North Sumatera

ABOUT THE AUTHOR

 Vivian Siahaan is a highly motivated individual with a passion for continuous learning and exploring new areas. Born and raised in Hinalang Bagasan, Balige, situated on the picturesque banks of Lake Toba, she completed her high school education at SMAN 1 Balige. Vivian's journey into the world of programming began with a deep dive into various languages such as Java, Android, JavaScript, CSS, C++, Python, R, Visual Basic, Visual C#, MATLAB, Mathematica, PHP, JSP, MySQL, SQL Server, Oracle, Access, and more. Starting from scratch, Vivian diligently studied programming, focusing on mastering the fundamental syntax and logic. She honed her skills by creating practical GUI applications, gradually building her expertise. One particular area of interest for Vivian is animation and game development, where she aspires to make significant contributions. Alongside her programming and mathematical pursuits, she also finds joy in indulging in novels, nurturing her love for literature. Vivian Siahaan's passion for programming and her extensive knowledge are reflected in the numerous ebooks she has authored. Her works, published by Sparta Publisher, cover a wide range of topics, including "Data Structure with Java," "Java Programming: Cookbook," "C++ Programming: Cookbook," "C Programming For High Schools/Vocational Schools and Students," "Java Programming for SMA/SMK," "Java Tutorial: GUI, Graphics and Animation," "Visual Basic Programming: From A to Z," "Java Programming for Animation and Games," "C# Programming for SMA/SMK and Students," "MATLAB For Students and Researchers," "Graphics in JavaScript: Quick Learning Series," "JavaScript Image Processing Methods: From A to Z," "Java GUI Case Study: AWT & Swing," "Basic CSS and JavaScript," "PHP/MySQL Programming: Cookbook," "Visual Basic: Cookbook," "C++ Programming for High Schools/Vocational Schools and Students," "Concepts and Practices of C++," "PHP/MySQL For Students," "C# Programming: From A to Z," "Visual Basic for SMA/SMK and Students," and "C# .NET and SQL Server for High School/Vocational School and Students." Furthermore, at the ANDI Yogyakarta publisher, Vivian Siahaan has contributed to several notable books, including "Python Programming Theory and Practice," "Python GUI Programming," "Python GUI and Database," "Build From Zero School Database Management System In Python/MySQL," "Database Management System in Python/MySQL," "Python/MySQL For Management Systems of Criminal Track Record Database," "Java/MySQL For Management Systems of Criminal Track Records Database," "Database and Cryptography Using Java/MySQL," and "Build From Zero School Database Management System With Java/MySQL." Vivian's diverse range of expertise in programming languages, combined with her passion for exploring new horizons, makes her a dynamic and versatile individual in the field of technology. Her dedication to learning, coupled with her strong analytical and problem-solving skills, positions her as a valuable asset in any programming endeavor. Vivian Siahaan's contributions to the world of programming and literature continue to inspire and empower aspiring programmers and readers alike.

 Rismon Hasiholan Sianipar, born in Pematang Siantar in 1994, is a distinguished researcher and expert in the field of electrical engineering. After completing his education at SMAN 3 Pematang Siantar, Rismon ventured to the city of Jogjakarta to pursue his academic journey. He obtained his Bachelor of Engineering (S.T) and Master of Engineering (M.T) degrees in Electrical Engineering from Gadjah Mada University in 1998 and 2001, respectively, under the guidance of esteemed professors, Dr. Adhi Soesanto and Dr. Thomas Sri Widodo. During his studies, Rismon focused on researching non-stationary signals and their energy analysis using time-frequency maps. He explored the dynamic nature of signal energy distribution on time-frequency maps and developed innovative techniques using discrete wavelet transformations to design non-linear filters for data pattern analysis. His research showcased the application of these techniques in various fields. In recognition of his academic prowess, Rismon was awarded the prestigious Monbukagakusho scholarship by the Japanese Government in 2003. He went on to pursue his Master of Engineering (M.Eng) and Doctor of Engineering (Dr.Eng) degrees at Yamaguchi University, supervised by Prof. Dr. Hidetoshi Miike. Rismon's master's and doctoral theses revolved around combining the SR-FHN (Stochastic Resonance Fitzhugh-Nagumo) filter strength with the cryptosystem ECC (elliptic curve cryptography) 4096-bit. This innovative approach effectively suppressed noise in digital images and videos while ensuring their authenticity. Rismon's research findings have been published in renowned international scientific journals, and his patents have been officially registered in Japan. Notably, one of his patents, with registration number 2008-009549, gained recognition. He actively collaborates with several universities and research institutions in Japan, specializing in cryptography, cryptanalysis, and digital forensics, particularly in the areas of audio, image, and video analysis. With a passion for knowledge sharing, Rismon has authored numerous national and international scientific articles and authored several national books. He has also actively participated in workshops related to cryptography, cryptanalysis, digital watermarking, and digital forensics. During these workshops, Rismon has assisted Prof. Hidetoshi Miike in developing applications related to digital image and video processing, steganography, cryptography, watermarking, and more, which serve as valuable training materials. Rismon's field of interest encompasses multimedia security, signal processing, digital image and video analysis, cryptography, digital communication, digital forensics, and data compression. He continues to advance his research by developing applications using programming languages such as Python, MATLAB, C++, C, VB.NET, C#.NET, R, and Java. These applications serve both research and commercial purposes, further contributing to the advancement of signal and image analysis. Rismon Hasiholan Sianipar is a dedicated researcher and expert in the field of electrical engineering, particularly in the areas of signal processing, cryptography, and digital forensics. His academic achievements, patented inventions, and extensive publications demonstrate his commitment to advancing knowledge in these fields. Rismon's contributions to academia and his collaborations with prestigious institutions in Japan have solidified his position as a respected figure in the scientific community. Through his ongoing research and development of innovative applications, Rismon continues to make significant contributions to the field of electrical engineering.

In this project, we embarked on a comprehensive journey through the world of machine learning and model evaluation. Our primary goal was to develop a Tkinter GUI and assess various machine learning models on a given dataset to identify the best-performing one. This process is essential in solving real-world problems, as it helps us select the most suitable algorithm for a specific task. By crafting this Tkinter-powered GUI, we provided an accessible and user-friendly interface for users engaging with machine learning models. It simplified intricate processes, allowing users to load data, select models, initiate training, and visualize results without necessitating code expertise or command-line operations. This GUI introduced a higher degree of usability and accessibility to the machine learning workflow, accommodating users with diverse levels of technical proficiency.

We began by loading and preprocessing the dataset, a fundamental step in any machine learning project. Proper data preprocessing involves tasks such as handling missing values, encoding categorical features, and scaling numerical attributes. These operations ensure that the data is in a format suitable for training and testing machine learning models.

Once our data was ready, we moved on to the model selection phase. We evaluated multiple machine learning algorithms, each with its strengths and weaknesses. The models we explored included Logistic Regression, Random Forest, K-Nearest Neighbors (KNN), Decision Trees, Gradient Boosting, Extreme Gradient Boosting (XGBoost), Multi-Layer Perceptron (MLP), and Support Vector Classifier (SVC).

For each model, we employed a systematic approach to find the best hyperparameters using grid search with cross-validation. This technique allowed us to explore different combinations of hyperparameters and select the configuration that yielded the highest accuracy on the training data. These hyperparameters included settings like the number of estimators, learning rate, and kernel function, depending on the specific model.

After obtaining the best hyperparameters for each model, we trained them on our preprocessed dataset. This training process involved using the training data to teach the model to make predictions on new, unseen examples. Once trained, the models were ready for evaluation.

We assessed the performance of each model using a set of well-established evaluation metrics. These metrics included accuracy, precision, recall, and F1-score. Accuracy measured the overall correctness of predictions, while precision quantified the proportion of true positive predictions out of all positive predictions. Recall, on the other hand, represented the proportion of true positive predictions out of all actual positives, highlighting a model's ability to identify positive cases. The F1-score combined precision and recall into a single metric, helping us gauge the overall balance between these two aspects.

To visualize the model's performance, we created key graphical representations. These included confusion matrices, which showed the number of true positive, true negative, false positive, and false negative predictions, aiding in understanding the model's classification results. Additionally, we generated Receiver Operating Characteristic (ROC) curves and area under the curve (AUC) scores, which depicted a model's ability to distinguish between classes. High AUC values indicated excellent model performance.

Furthermore, we constructed true values versus predicted values diagrams to provide insights into how well our models aligned with the actual data distribution. Learning curves were also generated to observe a model's performance as a function of training data size, helping us assess whether the model was overfitting or underfitting.

Lastly, we presented the results in a clear and organized manner, saving them to Excel files for easy reference. This allowed us to compare the performance of different models and make an informed choice about which one to select for our specific task.

In summary, this project was a comprehensive exploration of the machine learning model development and evaluation process. We prepared the data, selected and fine-tuned various models, assessed their performance using multiple metrics and visualizations, and ultimately arrived at a well-informed decision about the most suitable model for our dataset. This approach serves as a valuable blueprint for tackling real-world machine learning challenges effectively.

CONTENT

MACHINE LEARNING MODELS   **79**

TKINTER, DATA SCIENCE, AND MACHINE LEARNING

VIVIAN SIAHAAN
RISMON HASIHOLAN SIANIPAR

Published: AGUST 2023
Production reference: 4280123
Published by BALIGE Publishing Ltd.
BALIGE, North Sumatera

ABOUT THE AUTHOR

Vivian Siahaan is a highly motivated individual with a passion for continuous learning and exploring new areas. Born and raised in Hinalang Bagasan, Balige, situated on the picturesque banks of Lake Toba, she completed her high school education at SMAN 1 Balige. Vivian's journey into the world of programming began with a deep dive into various languages such as Java, Android, JavaScript, CSS, C++, Python, R, Visual Basic, Visual C#, MATLAB, Mathematica, PHP, JSP, MySQL, SQL Server, Oracle, Access, and more. Starting from scratch, Vivian diligently studied programming, focusing on mastering the fundamental syntax and logic. She honed her skills by creating practical GUI applications, gradually building her expertise. One particular area of interest for Vivian is animation and game development, where she aspires to make significant contributions. Alongside her programming and mathematical pursuits, she also finds joy in indulging in novels, nurturing her love for literature. Vivian Siahaan's passion for programming and her extensive knowledge are reflected in the numerous ebooks she has authored. Her works, published by Sparta Publisher, cover a wide range of topics, including "Data Structure with Java," "Java Programming: Cookbook," "C++ Programming: Cookbook," "C Programming For High Schools/Vocational Schools and Students," "Java Programming for SMA/SMK," "Java Tutorial: GUI, Graphics and Animation," "Visual Basic Programming: From A to Z," "Java Programming for Animation and Games," "C# Programming for SMA/SMK and Students," "MATLAB For Students and Researchers," "Graphics in JavaScript: Quick Learning Series," "JavaScript Image Processing Methods: From A to Z," "Java GUI Case Study: AWT & Swing," "Basic CSS and JavaScript," "PHP/MySQL Programming: Cookbook," "Visual Basic: Cookbook," "C++ Programming for High Schools/Vocational Schools and Students," "Concepts and Practices of C++," "PHP/MySQL For Students," "C# Programming: From A to Z," "Visual Basic for SMA/SMK and Students," and "C# .NET and SQL Server for High School/Vocational School and Students." Furthermore, at the ANDI Yogyakarta publisher, Vivian Siahaan has contributed to several notable books, including "Python Programming Theory and Practice," "Python GUI Programming," "Python GUI and Database," "Build From Zero School Database Management System In Python/MySQL," "Database Management System in Python/MySQL," "Python/MySQL For Management Systems of Criminal Track Record Database," "Java/MySQL For Management Systems of Criminal Track Records Database," "Database and Cryptography Using Java/MySQL," and "Build From Zero School Database Management System With Java/MySQL." Vivian's diverse range of expertise in programming languages, combined with her passion for exploring new horizons, makes her a dynamic and versatile individual in the field of technology. Her dedication to learning, coupled with her strong analytical and problem-solving skills, positions her as a valuable asset in any programming endeavor. Vivian Siahaan's contributions to the world of programming and literature continue to inspire and empower aspiring programmers and readers alike.

Rismon Hasiholan Sianipar, born in Pematang Siantar in 1994, is a distinguished researcher and expert in the field of electrical engineering. After completing his education at SMAN 3 Pematang Siantar, Rismon ventured to the city of Jogjakarta to pursue his academic journey. He obtained his Bachelor of Engineering (S.T) and Master of Engineering (M.T) degrees in Electrical Engineering from Gadjah Mada University in 1998 and 2001, respectively, under the guidance of esteemed professors, Dr. Adhi Soesanto and Dr. Thomas Sri Widodo. During his studies, Rismon focused on researching non-stationary signals and their energy analysis using time-frequency maps. He explored the dynamic nature of signal energy distribution on time-frequency maps and developed innovative techniques using discrete wavelet transformations to design non-linear filters for data pattern analysis. His research showcased the application of these techniques in various fields. In recognition of his academic prowess, Rismon was awarded the prestigious Monbukagakusho scholarship by the Japanese Government in 2003. He went on to pursue his Master of Engineering (M.Eng) and Doctor of Engineering (Dr.Eng) degrees at Yamaguchi University, supervised by Prof. Dr. Hidetoshi Miike. Rismon's master's and doctoral theses revolved around combining the SR-FHN (Stochastic Resonance Fitzhugh-Nagumo) filter strength with the cryptosystem ECC (elliptic curve cryptography) 4096-bit. This innovative approach effectively suppressed noise in digital images and videos while ensuring their authenticity. Rismon's research findings have been published in renowned international scientific journals, and his patents have been officially registered in Japan. Notably, one of his patents, with registration number 2008-009549, gained recognition. He actively collaborates with several universities and research institutions in Japan, specializing in cryptography, cryptanalysis, and digital forensics, particularly in the areas of audio, image, and video analysis. With a passion for knowledge sharing, Rismon has authored numerous national and international scientific articles and authored several national books. He has also actively participated in workshops related to cryptography, cryptanalysis, digital watermarking, and digital forensics. During these workshops, Rismon has assisted Prof. Hidetoshi Miike in developing applications related to digital image and video processing, steganography, cryptography, watermarking, and more, which serve as valuable training materials. Rismon's field of interest encompasses multimedia security, signal processing, digital image and video analysis, cryptography, digital communication, digital forensics, and data compression. He continues to advance his research by developing applications using programming languages such as Python, MATLAB, C++, C, VB.NET, C#.NET, R, and Java. These applications serve both research and commercial purposes, further contributing to the advancement of signal and image analysis. Rismon Hasiholan Sianipar is a dedicated researcher and expert in the field of electrical engineering, particularly in the areas of signal processing, cryptography, and digital forensics. His academic achievements, patented inventions, and extensive publications demonstrate his commitment to advancing knowledge in these fields. Rismon's contributions to academia and his collaborations with prestigious institutions in Japan have solidified his position as a respected figure in the scientific community. Through his ongoing research and development of innovative applications, Rismon continues to make significant contributions to the field of electrical engineering.

ABOUT THE BOOK

In this project, we embarked on a comprehensive journey through the world of machine learning and model evaluation. Our primary goal was to develop a Tkinter GUI and assess various machine learning models on a given dataset to identify the best-performing one. This process is essential in solving real-world problems, as it helps us select the most suitable algorithm for a specific task. By crafting this Tkinter-powered GUI, we provided an accessible and user-friendly interface for users engaging with machine learning models. It simplified intricate processes, allowing users to load data, select models, initiate training, and visualize results without necessitating code expertise or command-line operations. This GUI introduced a higher degree of usability and accessibility to the machine learning workflow, accommodating users with diverse levels of technical proficiency.

We began by loading and preprocessing the dataset, a fundamental step in any machine learning project. Proper data preprocessing involves tasks such as handling missing values, encoding categorical features, and scaling numerical attributes. These operations ensure that the data is in a format suitable for training and testing machine learning models.

Once our data was ready, we moved on to the model selection phase. We evaluated multiple machine learning algorithms, each with its strengths and weaknesses. The models we explored included Logistic Regression, Random Forest, K-Nearest Neighbors (KNN), Decision Trees, Gradient Boosting, Extreme Gradient Boosting (XGBoost), Multi-Layer Perceptron (MLP), and Support Vector Classifier (SVC).

For each model, we employed a systematic approach to find the best hyperparameters using grid search with cross-validation. This technique allowed us to explore different combinations of hyperparameters and select the configuration that yielded the highest accuracy on the training data. These hyperparameters included settings like the number of estimators, learning rate, and kernel function, depending on the specific model.

After obtaining the best hyperparameters for each model, we trained them on our preprocessed dataset. This training process involved using the training data to teach the model to make predictions on new, unseen examples. Once trained, the models were ready for evaluation.

We assessed the performance of each model using a set of well-established evaluation metrics. These metrics included accuracy, precision, recall, and F1-score. Accuracy measured the overall correctness of predictions, while precision quantified the proportion of true positive predictions out of all positive predictions. Recall, on the other hand, represented the proportion of true positive predictions out of all actual positives, highlighting a model's ability to identify positive cases. The F1-score combined precision and recall into a single metric, helping us gauge the overall balance between these two aspects.

To visualize the model's performance, we created key graphical representations. These included confusion matrices, which showed the number of true positive, true negative, false positive, and false negative predictions, aiding in understanding the model's classification results. Additionally, we generated Receiver Operating Characteristic (ROC) curves and area under the curve (AUC) scores, which depicted a model's ability to distinguish between classes. High AUC values indicated excellent model performance.

Furthermore, we constructed true values versus predicted values diagrams to provide insights into how well our models aligned with the actual data distribution. Learning curves were also generated to observe a model's performance as a function of training data size, helping us assess whether the model was overfitting or underfitting.

Lastly, we presented the results in a clear and organized manner, saving them to Excel files for easy reference. This allowed us to compare the performance of different models and make an informed choice about which one to select for our specific task.

In summary, this project was a comprehensive exploration of the machine learning model development and evaluation process. We prepared the data, selected and fine-tuned various models, assessed their performance using multiple metrics and visualizations, and ultimately arrived at a well-informed decision about the most suitable model for our dataset. This approach serves as a valuable blueprint for tackling real-world machine learning challenges effectively.

CONTENT

MACHINE LEARNING MODELS — 79

FEATURES DISTRIBUTION AND DATA VISUALIZATION

Main Class

Open a new python file and save it as **main_class.py**. Then, import two libraries as follows:

```
#main_class.py
import tkinter as tk
from tkinter import *
```

These two lines of code import the tkinter library in Python and make its classes and functions accessible for use in your script. Let's break down these lines:

1. import tkinter as tk:
    This line imports the entire tkinter library and assigns it the alias "tk." Using an alias is a common practice to make code shorter and more readable, especially when you need to access various classes and functions from the imported library.
2. from tkinter import *:
    This line imports all the classes and functions from the tkinter library into your script's namespace. The asterisk * is a wildcard that represents all the elements in the tkinter library. It allows you to use tkinter classes and functions directly without prefixing them with "tk."

Together, these two lines provide access to the tkinter library, which is used for creating graphical user interfaces (GUI) in Python applications. With tkinter, you can create windows, buttons, labels, text boxes, and other GUI elements to build interactive desktop applications.

Defining Main Class

Create a basic graphical user interface (GUI) application using the tkinter library. Let's break down the code:

1. Class Definition - **Main_Class**:

```
class Main_Class:
```

```
def __init__(self, root):
    self.initialize()
```

This defines a class named **Main_Class**. It has a constructor (__init__) that takes two arguments: self and root. self is a reference to the instance of the class being created, and root is expected to be a tkinter Tk instance (the main application window).

2. Initialization Method – initialize():

```
def initialize(self):
    self.root = root
    width = 1500
    height = 750
    self.root.geometry(f"{width}x{height}")
    self.root.title("TKINTER AND DATA SCIENCE")
```

- The initialize() method is called within the class's constructor and is responsible for setting up the main application window.
- It assigns the root (main tkinter window) to self.root, making it accessible within the class.
- It sets the width and height of the window to 1500x750 pixels using the geometry method.
- It sets the title of the window to "TKINTER AND DATA SCIENCE" using the title method.

3. Main Execution Block:

```
if __name__ == "__main__":
    root = tk.Tk()
    app = Main_Class(root)
    root.mainloop()
```

- This block checks if the script is being run as the main program (not imported as a module).
- It creates a tkinter Tk instance called root, which represents the main application window.
- It then creates an instance of the Main_Class class and passes the root window as an argument.
- Finally, it enters the main event loop using root.mainloop(), which keeps the application running and responsive to user interactions.

In summary, this code defines a basic tkinter-based GUI application with a main window. The **Main_Class** class is used to encapsulate the window initialization logic. When the script is run, it creates the main window, configures it, and enters the tkinter event loop, allowing the GUI to be displayed and interacted with by the user.

Design_Window Class

Create a new python file named **design_window.py**. This class is intended to encapsulate the design and layout of a graphical user interface (GUI) window using the tkinter library.

```python
#design_window.py
import tkinter as tk
from tkinter import ttk
from matplotlib.figure import Figure
from matplotlib.backends.backend_tkagg import FigureCanvasTkAgg

class Design_Window:
    def add_widgets(self, root):
        #Adds button(s)
        self.add_buttons(root)

        #Adds canvasses
        self.add_canvas(root)

        #Adds labels
        self.add_labels(root)

        #Adds listbox widget
        self.add_listboxes(root)

        #Adds combobox widget
        self.add_comboboxes(root)
```

In summary, the Design_Window class is to provide a structured way to add various GUI elements (buttons, canvases, labels, listboxes, and comboboxes) to a tkinter window. The organization of these elements is intended to create a user-friendly and functional graphical interface for an application. However, to fully understand how these widgets are configured and arranged, you would need to refer to the actual code in **design_window.py**.

Adding Buttons

The code defines a method named add_buttons () within Design_Window class. It adds two buttons to tkinter GUI window:

```
def add_buttons(self, root):
    #Adds button
    self.button1 = tk.Button(root, height=2, width=30, text="LOAD DATASET")
    self.button1.grid(row=0, column=0, padx=5, pady=5, sticky="w")

    self.button2 = tk.Button(root, height=2, width=30, text="SPLIT DATA")
    self.button2.grid(row=9, column=0, padx=5, pady=5, sticky="w")
```

Let's break down how these buttons are created and placed within the window:

1. add_buttons() Method:
   - This method is responsible for adding buttons to the tkinter window.
   - It takes two arguments: self (a reference to the instance of the Design_Window class) and root (the tkinter main window to which the buttons will be added).
2. Adding Buttons:
   Two buttons are added within this method using tk.Button(root, height=2, width=30, text="BUTTON_TEXT"), where:
   - root is the tkinter window where the buttons will be placed.
   - height=2 sets the height of the button (in text lines) to 2 units.
   - width=30 sets the width of the button (in characters) to 30 units.
   - text="BUTTON_TEXT" sets the text label displayed on the button to "BUTTON_TEXT."
3. Grid Placement:
   - The grid() method is used to specify the row and column placement of each button within the tkinter window.
   - For self.button1, it is placed in row 0, column 0 of the grid. padx and pady specify padding (space) around the button, and sticky indicates how the button sticks to the grid cell (in this case, "w" means west, or left-aligned).
   - For self.button2, it is placed in row 9, column 0 with similar padding and alignment settings.

These buttons, once created and placed, will appear as interactive elements within the tkinter window. Users can click on them to trigger specific actions associated with each button. The buttons are labeled "LOAD DATASET" and "SPLIT DATA," respectively, indicating their functions in the GUI application.

Adding Labels

The code defines a method named add_labels() within Design_Window class, part of the tkinter GUI application. This method is responsible for adding labels (text labels) to the GUI window.

```
def add_labels(self, root):
```

```
#Adds labels
self.label1 = tk.Label(root, text = "CHOOSE PLOT", fg = "red")
self.label1.grid(row=1, column=0, padx=5, pady=1, sticky="w")

self.label2 = tk.Label(root, text = "CHOOSE CATEGORIZED PLOT", fg = "blue")
self.label2.grid(row=3, column=0, padx=5, pady=1, sticky="w")

self.label3 = tk.Label(root, text = "CHOOSE FEATURES", fg = "black")
self.label3.grid(row=5, column=0, padx=5, pady=1, sticky="w")

self.label4 = tk.Label(root, text = "CHOOSE REGRESSORS", fg = "green")
self.label4.grid(row=7, column=0, padx=5, pady=1, sticky="w")

self.label5 = tk.Label(root, text = "CHOOSE MACHINE LEARNING", fg = "blue")
self.label5.grid(row=10, column=0, padx=5, pady=1, sticky="w")

self.label6 = tk.Label(root, text = "CHOOSE DEEP LEARNING", fg = "red")
self.label6.grid(row=12, column=0, padx=5, pady=1, sticky="w")
```

Let's break down how these labels are created and placed within the tkinter window:
1. add_labels() Method:
    - This method is designed to add labels to the tkinter window.
    - It takes two arguments: self (a reference to the instance of the class) and root (the tkinter main window to which the labels will be added).
2. Adding Labels:
    Multiple labels are created within this method using tk.Label(root, text="LABEL_TEXT", fg="COLOR"), where:
    - root is the tkinter window where the labels will be placed.
    - text="LABEL_TEXT" sets the text content of the label to "LABEL_TEXT."
    - fg="COLOR" sets the foreground color (text color) of the label to a specified color (e.g., "red," "blue," "green," or "black").
3. Grid Placement:
    - The grid() method is used to specify the row and column placement of each label within the tkinter window grid.
    - Each label is placed in a specific row and column, with optional padding (padx and pady) and alignment (sticky) settings.

Here's a breakdown of where each label is placed in the grid:
- self.label1 is placed in row 1, column 0.
- self.label2 is placed in row 3, column 0.
- self.label3 is placed in row 5, column 0.

- self.label4 is placed in row 7, column 0.
- self.label5 is placed in row 10, column 0.
- self.label6 is placed in row 12, column 0.

These labels serve as descriptive text elements within the tkinter window, providing instructions or information to the user about the different options or features available in the GUI application. The colors are used to distinguish the labels and make them visually appealing or to categorize them based on their purpose or function.

Adding Figures and Canvases

The code defines a method named add_canvas() within Design_Window class. This method is responsible for adding canvas widgets to a tkinter GUI window.

```
def add_canvas(self, root):
    #Menambahkan canvas1 widget pada root untuk menampilkan hasil
    self.figure1 = Figure(figsize=(6.2, 7), dpi=100)
    self.figure1.patch.set_facecolor("lightgray")
    self.canvas1 = FigureCanvasTkAgg(self.figure1, master=root)
    self.canvas1.get_tk_widget().grid(row=0, column=1, columnspan=1,
        rowspan=25, padx=5, pady=5, sticky="n")

    #Menambahkan canvas2 widget pada root untuk menampilkan hasil
    self.figure2 = Figure(figsize=(6.2, 7), dpi=100)
    self.figure2.patch.set_facecolor("lightgray")
    self.canvas2 = FigureCanvasTkAgg(self.figure2, master=root)
    self.canvas2.get_tk_widget().grid(row=0, column=2, columnspan=1,
        rowspan=25, padx=5, pady=5, sticky="n")
```

Let's break down the code:
1. add_canvas() Method:
    - This method is designed to add canvas widgets to the tkinter window.
    - It takes two arguments: self (a reference to the instance of the class) and root (the tkinter main window to which the canvas widgets will be added).
2. Adding Canvas Widgets:
   Two canvas widgets are added within this method. Both are used to display graphical results.
3. Creating Figure Objects:
    - For each canvas, a Figure object is created. A Figure in matplotlib is a top-level container for all plot elements.

- The Figure objects are configured with specific dimensions and a background color. The figsize parameter sets the width and height of the figure, and dpi (dots per inch) determines the resolution of the figure.
- The patch.set_facecolor method is used to set the background color of the figure (canvas) to "lightgray."

4. Creating Canvas Widgets:
    - For each canvas, a FigureCanvasTkAgg object is created. This object associates a Figure with a tkinter canvas widget.
    - self.canvas1 represents the first canvas, and self.canvas2 represents the second canvas.
    - The FigureCanvasTkAgg constructor takes two arguments: the Figure object and the master (root) tkinter window.

5. Grid Placement:
    - The grid method is used to specify the row and column placement of each canvas widget within the tkinter window grid.
    - Both canvas widgets are placed in specific rows and columns, with optional padding (padx and pady) and alignment (sticky) settings.
    - They are placed side by side in different columns of the same row, suggesting a horizontal layout.

In summary, this method adds two canvas widgets to the tkinter window, each capable of displaying graphical results. The canvas widgets are associated with Figure objects, allowing for the rendering of various types of plots or graphical content within the GUI. The background color of the canvases is set to "lightgray" for visual clarity.

Adding ListBox

The code defines a method named add_listboxes() within the Design_Window class. This method is responsible for adding a listbox widget to a tkinter GUI window and populating it with a list of items.

```python
def add_listboxes(self, root):
    #Menambahkan list widget
    self.listbox = tk.Listbox(root, selectmode=tk.SINGLE, width=35)
    self.listbox.grid(row=2, column=0, sticky='n', padx=5, pady=1)

    # Menyisipkan item ke dalam list widget
    items = ["Marital Status", "Education", "Country",
        "Age Group", "Education with Response 0",
        "Education with Response 1",
        "Country with Response 0", "Country with Response 1",
        "Customer Age", "Income", "Amount of Wines",
```

```
        "Education versus Response", "Age Group versus Response",
        "Marital Status versus Response", "Country versus Response",
        "Number of Dependants versus Response",
        "Country versus Customer Age Per Education",
        "Num_TotalPurchases versus Education Per Marital Status"]
    for item in items:
        self.listbox.insert(tk.END, item)

    self.listbox.config(height=len(items))
```

Let's break down the code:
1. add_listboxes() Method:
    *   This method is designed to add a listbox widget to a tkinter window.
    *   It takes two arguments: self (a reference to the instance of the class) and root (the tkinter main window to which the listbox will be added).
2. Adding the Listbox Widget:
    A listbox widget is created using tk.Listbox(root, selectmode=tk.SINGLE, width=35), where:
    *   root is the tkinter window where the listbox will be placed.
    *   selectmode=tk.SINGLE specifies that only one item can be selected at a time.
    *   width=35 sets the width of the listbox widget to 35 characters.
3. Grid Placement:
    *   The grid() method is used to specify the row and column placement of the listbox widget within the tkinter window grid.
    *   The listbox is placed in row 2, column 0, with optional padding (padx and pady) and alignment (sticky) settings.
4. Populating the Listbox:
    *   A list of items (strings) is defined in the items list variable. These items represent the options that will be displayed in the listbox.
    *   A loop iterates through each item in the items list and inserts it into the listbox using the insert method with tk.END as the index, which adds each item to the end of the listbox.
5. Configuring the Listbox Height:
    The config() method is used to configure the height of the listbox to match the number of items in the items list. This ensures that all items are visible within the listbox without the need for scrolling.

In summary, this method adds a listbox widget to the tkinter window, allowing the user to select one item from a predefined list of options. The listbox is populated with items, and its height is adjusted to accommodate all the items without scrolling. This is commonly used in GUIs to provide users with a selection of choices.

Adding Comboboxes

The code defines a method named add_comboboxes() within Design_Window class. This method is responsible for adding combo box (combobox) widgets to a tkinter GUI window and populating them with lists of options.

```python
def add_comboboxes(self, root):
    # Create ComboBoxes
    self.combo1 = ttk.Combobox(root, width=32)
    self.combo1["values"] = ["Categorized Income versus Response",
        "Categorized Total Purchase versus Categorized Income",
        "Categorized Recency versus Categorized Total Purchase",
        "Categorized Customer Month versus Categorized Customer Age",
        "Categorized Amount of Gold Products versus Categorized Income",
        "Categorized Amount of Fish Products versus Categorized Total AmountSpent",
        "Categorized Amount of Meat Products versus Categorized Recency",
        "Distribution of Numerical Columns"]
    self.combo1.grid(row=4, column=0, padx=5, pady=1, sticky="n")

    self.combo2 = ttk.Combobox(root, width=32)
    self.combo2["values"] = ["Correlation Matrix", "RF Features Importance",
        "ET Features Importance", "RFE Features Importance"]
    self.combo2.grid(row=6, column=0, padx=5, pady=1, sticky="n")

    self.combo3 = ttk.Combobox(root, width=32)
    self.combo3["values"] = ["Linear Regression", "RF Regression",
        "Decision Trees Regression", "KNN Regression",
        "AdaBoost Regression", "Gradient Boosting Regression",
        "XGB Regression", "LGB Regression", "CatBoost Regression",
        "SVR Regression", "Lasso Regression", "Ridge Regression"]
    self.combo3.grid(row=8, column=0, padx=5, pady=1, sticky="n")

    self.combo4 = ttk.Combobox(root, width=32)
    self.combo4["values"] = ["Logistic Regression", "Random Forest",
        "Decision Trees", "K-Nearest Neighbors",
        "AdaBoost", "Gradient Boosting",
        "Extreme Gradient Boosting", "Light Gradient Boosting",
        "Multi-Layer Perceptron", "Support Vector Classifier"]
    self.combo4.grid(row=11, column=0, padx=5, pady=1, sticky="n")
```

Let's break down the code:
1. add_comboboxes() Method:
    - This method is designed to add combo box (combobox) widgets to a tkinter window.
    - It takes two arguments: self (a reference to the instance of the class) and root (the tkinter main window to which the comboboxes will be added).

2. Adding Combo Boxes:
   - Multiple comboboxes are created within this method, each corresponding to a specific set of options.
   - Each combobox is created using ttk.Combobox(root, width=32), where:
     - root is the tkinter window where the combobox will be placed.
     - width=32 sets the width of the combobox widget to 32 characters.
3. Populating Combo Boxes:
   - Each combobox is populated with a list of values (options) using the "values" attribute.
   - The options are provided as lists of strings, such as ["Option 1", "Option 2", ...].
4. Grid Placement:
   - The grid method is used to specify the row and column placement of each combobox widget within the tkinter window grid.
   - Each combobox is placed in a specific row and column, with optional padding (padx and pady) and alignment (sticky) settings.

Here's a breakdown of where each combobox is placed in the grid:
- self.combo1 is placed in row 4, column 0.
- self.combo2 is placed in row 6, column 0.
- self.combo3 is placed in row 8, column 0.
- self.combo4 is placed in row 11, column 0.

Each combobox provides a dropdown list of options for the user to choose from. These comboboxes allow users to select various analysis or modeling options in the GUI application, making it interactive and versatile.

Adding Widgets onto Root Window

Add statement import in Main_Class, **from design_window import Design_Window**. It's used to import the Design_Window class from the design_window module into your current Python script or program. Let's break down what this statement does:
- from design_window: This part specifies the name of the module (Python file) that you want to import from. In this case, it's design_window.
- import Design_Window: After specifying the module, you use the import keyword to indicate that you want to import something from that module. Here, you're importing the Design_Window class.

So, after executing this import statement, you will have access to the Design_Window class in Main_Class script. You can create instances of this class and use its methods and attributes as needed.

Then, create an instance of the Design_Window class and then adding widgets to it. Put these code inside initialize() method in Main_Class:

```
#Creates necessary objects
self.obj_window = Design_Window()

#Places widgets in root
self.obj_window.add_widgets(self.root)
```

Let's break down what this code does:

1. Creating an Instance of Design_Window:
    self.obj_window = Design_Window(): This line creates an instance of the Design_Window class and assigns it to the variable self.obj_window. This instance represents a GUI window where you can add widgets.
2. Adding Widgets to the Design_Window:
    *   self.obj_window.add_widgets(self.root): Here, you are calling the add_widgets() method of the Design_Window instance (self.obj_window) and passing self.root as an argument.
    *   The add_widgets method is expected to add various widgets (buttons, labels, listboxes, comboboxes, etc.) to the Design_Window instance (self.obj_window).

By creating an instance of Design_Window and adding widgets to it, you are organizing your GUI components within the Design_Window object. This can help keep your code modular and make it easier to manage the layout and functionality of your GUI application.

Now, the main_class.py is as follows:

```
#main_class.py
import tkinter as tk
from tkinter import *
from design_window import Design_Window
import os

class Main_Class:
    def __init__(self, root):
        self.initialize()

    def initialize(self):
        self.root = root
        width = 1500
        height = 750
        self.root.geometry(f"{width}x{height}")
```

```
    self.root.title("TKINTER AND DATA SCIENCE")

    #Creates necessary objects
    self.obj_window = Design_Window()

    #Places widgets in root
    self.obj_window.add_widgets(self.root)

if __name__ == "__main__":
    root = tk.Tk()
    app = Main_Class(root)
    root.mainloop()
```

Run main_class.py. You will see all widgets displayed in root window as shown in figure 1.

Figure 1 All widgets now are placed in root window

Process_Data Class
Create a new python file named process_data.py.

```
#process_data.py
import os
import numpy as np
import pandas as pd
from sklearn.preprocessing import LabelEncoder
from sklearn.ensemble import RandomForestClassifier, ExtraTreesClassifier
from sklearn.linear_model import LogisticRegression
```

from sklearn.feature_selection import RFE

Let's break down the key elements of this script:
1. Imports:
    *   os: The os module provides a portable way of using operating system-dependent functionality. It's often used for file and directory operations.
    *   numpy as np: This imports the popular numerical library NumPy with the alias np, which is a common convention.
    *   pandas as pd: This imports the Pandas library with the alias pd. Pandas is commonly used for data manipulation and analysis.
    *   LabelEncoder from sklearn.preprocessing: LabelEncoder is used for encoding categorical labels into numerical values.
    *   RandomForestClassifier and ExtraTreesClassifier from sklearn.ensemble: These are machine learning models for classification tasks using Random Forests and Extra Trees.
    *   LogisticRegression from sklearn.linear_model: This is a machine learning model for classification using logistic regression.
    *   RFE (Recursive Feature Elimination) from sklearn.feature_selection: RFE is used for feature selection in machine learning.
2. Data Processing and Machine Learning Libraries:
    The script focuses on data processing and machine learning tasks, as it imports libraries for data manipulation (numpy and pandas) and machine learning (sklearn).
3. Machine Learning Algorithms:
    The script imports several machine learning algorithms such as Random Forest, Extra Trees, and Logistic Regression. These algorithms are to be used for building and training classification models.
4. Feature Selection:
    The import of RFE (Recursive Feature Elimination) from sklearn.feature_selection suggests that feature selection techniques are used to choose relevant features for machine learning models.
5. Data Encoding:
    The LabelEncoder from sklearn.preprocessing is often used to encode categorical data into numerical format, which is required by many machine learning algorithms.
6. Data Processing and Manipulation:
    The numpy and pandas libraries are commonly used for data processing and manipulation tasks. These libraries provide efficient data structures and functions for working with large datasets.

Reading Dataset

In process_data.py, create a class named Process_Data. Then, defines a new methode named read_dataset():

```
class Process_Data:
    def read_dataset(self, filename):
        #Reads dataset
        curr_path = os.getcwd()
        path = os.path.join(curr_path, filename)
        df = pd.read_csv(path)

        return df
```

The code defines a method named read_dataset() within a Python class called Process_Data. This method is responsible for reading a dataset from a CSV file and returning it as a Pandas DataFrame. Let's break down what this method does:

1. Method Definition:

   def read_dataset(self, filename): This defines the read_dataset() method, which takes two arguments: self (a reference to the instance of the class) and filename (the name of the CSV file to be read).

2. File Path Construction:

   • curr_path = os.getcwd(): This line retrieves the current working directory using the os.getcwd() function and stores it in the variable curr_path.

   • path = os.path.join(curr_path, filename): Here, the script constructs the full path to the CSV file by joining the curr_path (current working directory) and the provided filename. This ensures that the file can be located and read.

3. Reading the CSV File:

   • df = pd.read_csv(path): This line uses the Pandas library's read_csv() function to read the CSV file located at the path generated in the previous step. The data from the CSV file is loaded into a Pandas DataFrame, and that DataFrame is assigned to the variable df.

4. Returning the DataFrame:

   return df: Finally, the method returns the Pandas DataFrame containing the data from the CSV file.

This read_dataset() method is designed to be part of a data processing workflow. It allows you to read datasets from CSV files, making it convenient for further data analysis and manipulation. You can call this method on an instance of the Process_Data class to read a dataset and work with its contents.

Preprocessing Data

The code defines a method named preprocess() within Process_Data class. This method is responsible for preprocessing a dataset read from a CSV file named "marketing_data.csv."

```python
def preprocess(self):
    df = self.read_dataset("marketing_data.csv")

    #Drops ID column
    df = df.drop("ID", axis = 1)

    #Renames column name and corrects data type
    df.rename(columns={' Income ':'Income'},inplace=True)
    df["Dt_Customer"] = pd.to_datetime(df["Dt_Customer"], format='%m/%d/%y')
    df["Income"] = df["Income"].str.replace("$","").str.replace(",","")
    df["Income"] = df["Income"].astype(float)

    #Checks null values
    print(df.isnull().sum())
    print('Total number of null values: ', df.isnull().sum().sum())

    #Imputes Income column with median values
    df['Income'] = df['Income'].fillna(df['Income'].median())
    print(f'Number of Null values in "Income" after Imputation: {df["Income"].isna().sum()}')

    #Transformasi Dt_Customer
    df['Dt_Customer'] = pd.to_datetime(df['Dt_Customer'])
    print(f'After Transformation:\n{df["Dt_Customer"].head()}')
    df['Customer_Age'] = df['Dt_Customer'].dt.year - df['Year_Birth']

    #Creates number of children/dependents in home by adding 'Kidhome' and 'Teenhome' features
    #Creates number of Total_Purchases by adding all the purchases features
    #Creates TotalAmount_Spent by adding all the Mnt* features
    df['Dt_Customer_Month'] = df['Dt_Customer'].dt.month
    df['Dt_Customer_Year'] = df['Dt_Customer'].dt.year
    df['Num_Dependants'] = df['Kidhome'] + df['Teenhome']

    purchase_features = [c for c in df.columns if 'Purchase' in str(c)]
    #Removes 'NumDealsPurchases' from the list above
    purchase_features.remove('NumDealsPurchases')
    df['Num_TotalPurchases'] = df[purchase_features].sum(axis = 1)

    amt_spent_features = [c for c in df.columns if 'Mnt' in str(c)]
    df['TotalAmount_Spent'] = df[amt_spent_features].sum(axis = 1)

    #Creates a categorical feature using the customer's age by binnning them,
    #to help understanding purchasing behaviour
    print(f'Min. Customer Age: {df["Customer_Age"].min()}')
    print(f'Max. Customer Age: {df["Customer_Age"].max()}')
    df['AgeGroup'] = pd.cut(df['Customer_Age'], bins = [6, 24, 29, 40, 56, 75],
        labels = ['Gen-Z', 'Gen-Y.1', 'Gen-Y.2', 'Gen-X', 'BBoomers'])
```

```
return df
```

Let's break down what this method does step by step:
1. Reading the Dataset:
   df = self.read_dataset("marketing_data.csv"): This line calls the read_dataset() method to read the CSV file into a Pandas DataFrame named df.
2. Data Cleaning and Transformation:
   - df = df.drop("ID", axis=1): It drops the "ID" column from the DataFrame.
   - df.rename(columns={' Income ':'Income'}, inplace=True): It renames the " Income " column to "Income" and removes leading/trailing spaces.
   - df["Dt_Customer"] = pd.to_datetime(df["Dt_Customer"], format='%m/%d/%y'): It converts the "Dt_Customer" column to a datetime format.
   - df["Income"] = df["Income"].str.replace("$","").str.replace(",",""): It removes dollar signs and commas from the "Income" column and converts it to a float data type.
   - df['Income'] = df['Income'].fillna(df['Income'].median()): It fills missing values in the "Income" column with the median value.
   - df['Customer_Age'] = df['Dt_Customer'].dt.year - df['Year_Birth']: It calculates the customer's age based on the "Dt_Customer" and "Year_Birth" columns.
3. Checking for Missing Values:
   - print(df.isnull().sum()): It prints the count of missing values for each column.
   - print('Total number of null values: ', df.isnull().sum().sum()): It prints the total number of missing values in the entire DataFrame.
4. Creating New Features:
   The code creates several new features:
   - Num_Dependants by adding the "Kidhome" and "Teenhome" features.
   - Num_TotalPurchases by summing the purchase-related features.
   - TotalAmount_Spent by summing the "Mnt*" features.
   - AgeGroup by binning customer ages into categories based on predefined bins.
5. Printing Summary Information:
   - print(f'Min. Customer Age: {df["Customer_Age"].min()}'): It prints the minimum customer age.
   - print(f'Max. Customer Age: {df["Customer_Age"].max()}'): It prints the maximum customer age.
6. Returning the Processed DataFrame:
   return df: Finally, the method returns the Pandas DataFrame with the dataset after preprocessing.

This preprocess method is responsible for cleaning, transforming, and enhancing the dataset, making it ready for further analysis or machine learning tasks. It demonstrates common data preprocessing steps such as data type conversion, missing value handling, and feature engineering.

Categorizing Features

The code defines a method named categorize() within Process_Data class. This method is responsible for categorizing various numerical features in a Pandas DataFrame into predefined bins.

```python
def categorize(self, df):
    #Creates a dummy dataframe for visualization
    df_dummy=df.copy()

    #Categorizes Income feature
    labels = ['0-20k', '20k-30k', '30k-50k','50k-70k','70k-700k']
    df_dummy['Income'] = pd.cut(df_dummy['Income'],
        [0, 20000, 30000, 50000, 70000, 700000], labels=labels)

    #Categorizes TotalAmount_Spent feature
    labels = ['0-200', '200-500', '500-800','800-1000','1000-3000']
    df_dummy['TotalAmount_Spent'] = pd.cut(df_dummy['TotalAmount_Spent'],
        [0, 200, 500, 800, 1000, 3000], labels=labels)

    #Categorizes Num_TotalPurchases feature
    labels = ['0-5', '5-10', '10-15','15-25','25-35']
    df_dummy['Num_TotalPurchases'] = pd.cut(df_dummy['Num_TotalPurchases'],
        [0, 5, 10, 15, 25, 35], labels=labels)

    #Categorizes Dt_Customer_Year feature
    labels = ['2012', '2013', '2014']
    df_dummy['Dt_Customer_Year'] = pd.cut(df_dummy['Dt_Customer_Year'],
        [0, 2012, 2013, 2014], labels=labels)

    #Categorizes Dt_Customer_Month feature
    labels = ['0-3', '3-6', '6-9','9-12']
    df_dummy['Dt_Customer_Month'] = pd.cut(df_dummy['Dt_Customer_Month'],
        [0, 3, 6, 9, 12], labels=labels)

    #Categorizes Customer_Age feature
    labels = ['0-30', '30-40', '40-50', '40-60','60-120']
    df_dummy['Customer_Age'] = pd.cut(df_dummy['Customer_Age'],
        [0, 30, 40, 50, 60, 120], labels=labels)

    #Categorizes MntGoldProds feature
    labels = ['0-30', '30-50', '50-80', '80-100','100-400']
    df_dummy['MntGoldProds'] = pd.cut(df_dummy['MntGoldProds'],
```

```
  [0, 30, 50, 80, 100, 400], labels=labels)

#Categorizes MntSweetProducts feature
labels = ['0-10', '10-20', '20-40', '40-100','100-300']
df_dummy['MntSweetProducts'] = pd.cut(df_dummy['MntSweetProducts'],
  [0, 10, 20, 40, 100, 300], labels=labels)

#Categorizes MntFishProducts feature
labels = ['0-10', '10-20', '20-40', '40-100','100-300']
df_dummy['MntFishProducts'] = pd.cut(df_dummy['MntFishProducts'],
  [0, 10, 20, 40, 100, 300], labels=labels)

#Categorizes MntMeatProducts feature
labels = ['0-50', '50-100', '100-200', '200-500','500-2000']
df_dummy['MntMeatProducts'] = pd.cut(df_dummy['MntMeatProducts'],
  [0, 50, 100, 200, 500, 2000], labels=labels)

#Categorizes MntFruits feature
labels = ['0-10', '10-30', '30-50', '50-100','100-200']
df_dummy['MntFruits'] = pd.cut(df_dummy['MntFruits'],
  [0, 1, 30, 50, 100, 200], labels=labels)

#Categorizes MntWines feature
labels = ['0-100', '100-300', '300-500', '500-1000','1000-1500']
df_dummy['MntWines'] = pd.cut(df_dummy['MntWines'],
  [0, 100, 300, 500, 1000, 1500], labels=labels)

#Categorizes Recency feature
labels = ['0-10', '10-30', '30-50', '50-80','80-100']
df_dummy['Recency'] = pd.cut(df_dummy['Recency'],
  [0, 10, 30, 50, 80, 100], labels=labels)

return df_dummy
```

Let's break down what this method does:
1. Method Definition:
   def categorize(self, df): This defines the categorize() method, which takes two arguments: self (a reference to the instance of the class) and df (a Pandas DataFrame containing the data to be categorized).
2. Creating a Dummy DataFrame:
   df_dummy = df.copy(): A copy of the input DataFrame df is made and stored in df_dummy. This is done to keep the original DataFrame intact while performing the categorization.
3. Categorizing Features:
   The method categorizes various numerical features in the df_dummy DataFrame using the pd.cut() function. Each feature is binned into categories based on predefined bins, and the categorized values are stored back in the df_dummy DataFrame.

4. Feature Categories:
    Each feature is categorized into specific bins, and labels are assigned to the categories. For example, the "Income" feature is categorized into labels like '0-20k', '20k-30k', and so on.
5. Returning the Categorized DataFrame:
    return df_dummy: Finally, the method returns the Pandas DataFrame df_dummy containing the categorized data.

This categorize method is useful for converting numerical features into categorical features with meaningful labels. It's often used when you want to analyze data in groups or perform aggregations based on these categories. The categorized data can be further used for visualization and analysis.

Extracting Categorical and Numerical Features

The code defines a method named extract_cat_num_cols() within Process_Data class. It is responsible for extracting and categorizing the columns in a Pandas DataFrame into two lists: categorical columns and numerical columns.

```python
def extract_cat_num_cols(self, df):
    #Extracts categorical and numerical columns in dummy dataset
    cat_cols = [col for col in df.columns if
        (df[col].dtype == 'object') or (df[col].dtype.name == 'category')]
    num_cols = [col for col in df.columns if
        (df[col].dtype != 'object') and (df[col].dtype.name != 'category')]

    return cat_cols, num_cols
```

Let's break down how this method works:
1. Method Definition:
    def extract_cat_num_cols(self, df): This is a method definition that takes two parameters: self, which is a reference to the instance of the class, and df, which is expected to be a Pandas DataFrame.
2. Extracting Categorical Columns:
    cat_cols = [col for col in df.columns if (df[col].dtype == 'object') or (df[col].dtype.name == 'category')]: This list comprehension iterates through the columns in the DataFrame df and checks if a column has either the data type 'object' or the data type 'category'. If a column matches either of these conditions, it is considered a categorical column and is added to the cat_cols list.
3. Extracting Numerical Columns:
    num_cols = [col for col in df.columns if (df[col].dtype != 'object') and (df[col].dtype.name != 'category')]: Similarly, this list comprehension iterates through the columns in the DataFrame df and checks if a column does not have the data type 'object' and does not

have the data type 'category'. If a column matches these conditions, it is considered a numerical column and is added to the num_cols list.

4. Returning the Categorized Columns:

    return cat_cols, num_cols: Finally, the method returns two lists: cat_cols, which contains the names of categorical columns, and num_cols, which contains the names of numerical columns.

This method is useful for quickly identifying and separating columns based on their data types, which can be helpful for various data preprocessing and analysis tasks. For example, you may want to apply different encoding techniques to categorical columns and scaling methods to numerical columns when working with machine learning models.

Encoding Categorical Features

In Process_Data class, the encode_categorical_feats() method in the code is responsible for encoding categorical features in a Pandas DataFrame using Label Encoding.

```
def encode_categorical_feats(self, df, cat_cols):
    #Encodes categorical features in original dataset
    print(f'Features that needs to be Label Encoded: \n{cat_cols}')

    for c in cat_cols:
        lbl = LabelEncoder()
        lbl.fit(list(df[c].astype(str).values))
        df[c] = lbl.transform(list(df[c].astype(str).values))
    print('Label Encoding done..')
    return df
```

Let's break down how this method works:

1. Method Definition:

    def encode_categorical_feats(self, df, cat_cols): This is a method definition that takes three parameters: self, which is a reference to the instance of the class, df, which is a Pandas DataFrame, and cat_cols, which is a list of categorical columns to be encoded.

2. Printing Categorical Features:

    print(f'Features that need to be Label Encoded: \n{cat_cols}'): This line prints the names of the categorical features that are going to be label-encoded.

3. Label Encoding:

    The method then iterates through each categorical column specified in cat_cols:

    *   for c in cat_cols:: This loop iterates through the names of the categorical columns.
    *   lbl = LabelEncoder(): A new instance of the LabelEncoder class is created. The LabelEncoder is a preprocessing technique that assigns a unique integer to each category in a categorical feature.

- lbl.fit(list(df[c].astype(str).values)): The fit method of the LabelEncoder is called with the values of the current categorical column. It converts the column values to strings (in case they are not already) and fits the encoder to these values.
- df[c] = lbl.transform(list(df[c].astype(str).values)): The transform method of the LabelEncoder is applied to the current categorical column, converting its values to their corresponding integer labels.

4. Printing Confirmation:

   print('Label Encoding done..'): This line prints a message confirming that the label encoding process has been completed.

5. Returning the Encoded DataFrame:

   return df: Finally, the method returns the Pandas DataFrame df with the categorical features label-encoded.

Label encoding is a technique commonly used to convert categorical data into a numerical format that machine learning algorithms can work with. Each category is assigned a unique integer label. It is important to note that label encoding may introduce ordinal relationships between categories, which may not be appropriate for all categorical features. In some cases, one-hot encoding or other encoding methods may be preferred, depending on the nature of the data and the machine learning model being used.

Extracting Input and Output Variables

In Process_Data class, the extract_input_output_vars() method in the code is responsible for extracting the input variables (features) and the output variable (target) from a Pandas DataFrame.

```
def extract_input_output_vars(self, df):
    #Extracts output and input variables
    y = df['Response'].values # Target for the model
    X = df.drop(['Dt_Customer', 'Year_Birth', 'Response'], axis = 1)

    return X, y
```

Let's break down how this method works:

1. Method Definition:

   def extract_input_output_vars(self, df): This is a method definition that takes two parameters: self, which is a reference to the instance of the class, and df, which is a Pandas DataFrame containing the dataset.

2. Extracting the Output Variable:

   y = df['Response'].values: This line extracts the output variable, often referred to as the target variable, from the DataFrame df. It assumes that the target variable is named

"Response" in the DataFrame. The .values attribute converts the target column into a NumPy array, which is commonly used as the target for machine learning models.

3. Extracting the Input Variables:

   X = df.drop(['Dt_Customer', 'Year_Birth', 'Response'], axis=1): This line extracts the input variables (features) from the DataFrame df. It drops three columns from the DataFrame: "Dt_Customer," "Year_Birth," and "Response." These columns are removed from the input features, leaving the rest of the columns as the input variables.

4. Returning the Extracted Variables:

   - return X, y: Finally, the method returns two variables:
   - X: This contains the input variables (features) for the machine learning model.
   - y: This contains the output variable (target) that the model aims to predict.

This method is designed to facilitate the preparation of data for machine learning tasks. It separates the features (input variables) from the target variable, making it easier to use the data with various machine learning algorithms. Typically, in supervised machine learning, X represents the independent variables, and y represents the dependent variable that the model will predict.

Feature Importances Using Random Forest Classifier

In Process_Data class, The feat_importance_rf() method in the code is responsible for calculating and returning feature importances using a Random Forest classifier.

```python
def feat_importance_rf(self, X, y):
    names = X.columns
    rf = RandomForestClassifier()
    rf.fit(X, y)

    result_rf = pd.DataFrame()
    result_rf['Features'] = X.columns
    result_rf ['Values'] = rf.feature_importances_
    result_rf.sort_values('Values', inplace = True, ascending = False)

    return result_rf
```

Let's break down how this method works:

1. Method Definition:

   def feat_importance_rf(self, X, y): This is a method definition that takes three parameters: self, which is a reference to the instance of the class, X, which is a Pandas DataFrame containing the input features, and y, which is a NumPy array containing the target variable.

2. Extracting Feature Names:

names = X.columns: This line extracts the names of the input features (columns) from the DataFrame X and stores them in the names variable. These feature names will be used for labeling the feature importances.

3. Random Forest Classifier:

rf = RandomForestClassifier(): An instance of the RandomForestClassifier is created. The Random Forest classifier is a machine learning model known for its ability to assess feature importance by analyzing how much each feature contributes to the model's predictions.

4. Fitting the Model:

rf.fit(X, y): The Random Forest classifier is fitted to the input features (X) and the target variable (y). This means the model is trained on the provided data.

5. Creating a Result DataFrame:
   - result_rf = pd.DataFrame(): An empty Pandas DataFrame called result_rf is created to store the feature importances.
   - result_rf['Features'] = X.columns: A column named "Features" is created in the result_rf DataFrame, and it is populated with the names of the input features.
   - result_rf['Values'] = rf.feature_importances_: Another column named "Values" is created, and it is populated with the feature importances calculated by the Random Forest classifier. These values represent how much each feature contributes to the model's predictions.

6. Sorting Feature Importances:

result_rf.sort_values('Values', inplace=True, ascending=False): The result_rf DataFrame is sorted in descending order based on the feature importances. This means that the most important features will appear at the top of the DataFrame.

7. Returning the Result DataFrame:

return result_rf: Finally, the method returns the result_rf DataFrame, which contains feature names and their corresponding importances as calculated by the Random Forest classifier.

This method is useful for identifying which features have the most influence on the model's predictions, which can be valuable for feature selection and understanding the importance of various factors in a predictive model.

Feature Importances Using Extra Trees Classifier

In Process_Data class, the feat_importance_et() method in the code is responsible for calculating and returning feature importances using an Extra Trees classifier. This method can be used to understand the importance of different features in a dataset when building a machine learning model.

```
def feat_importance_et(self, X, y):
    model = ExtraTreesClassifier()
    model.fit(X, y)

    result_et = pd.DataFrame()
    result_et['Features'] = X.columns
    result_et ['Values'] = model.feature_importances_
    result_et.sort_values('Values', inplace=True, ascending =False)

    return result_et
```

Let's discuss how this method works:
1. Method Definition:
   def feat_importance_et(self, X, y): This method is defined to calculate feature importances using the Extra Trees classifier. It takes three parameters: self, which refers to the instance of the class, X, which is a Pandas DataFrame containing the input features, and y, which is a NumPy array containing the target variable (labels or classes).
2. Creating an Extra Trees Classifier:
   model = ExtraTreesClassifier(): An instance of the ExtraTreesClassifier is created. This classifier is used for feature selection and classification tasks. It is an ensemble learning method similar to the Random Forest, but it has some differences in how it constructs and selects decision trees.
3. Fitting the Model:
   model.fit(X, y): The Extra Trees classifier is fitted to the input features X and the target variable y. This step involves training the classifier on the provided data to learn patterns and relationships between features and the target variable.
4. Creating a Result DataFrame:
   • result_et = pd.DataFrame(): An empty Pandas DataFrame called result_et is created to store the feature importances.
   • result_et['Features'] = X.columns: A column named "Features" is added to the result_et DataFrame, and it contains the names of the input features.
   • result_et['Values'] = model.feature_importances_: Another column named "Values" is added to the result_et DataFrame, and it contains the feature importances calculated by the Extra Trees classifier. These importances represent how much each feature contributes to the model's predictive performance.
5. Sorting Feature Importances:
   result_et.sort_values('Values', inplace=True, ascending=False): The result_et DataFrame is sorted based on the "Values" column in descending order. This means that the most important features will appear at the top of the DataFrame.

6. Returning the Result DataFrame:

   return result_et: Finally, the method returns the result_et DataFrame, which contains the feature names and their corresponding importances as calculated by the Extra Trees classifier.

The feature importances calculated by this method can be valuable for feature selection, dimensionality reduction, and gaining insights into which features are most influential in making predictions with machine learning models.

Feature Importances Using Recursive Feature Elimination (RFE)

In Process_Data class, the feat_importance_rfe() method in the code is responsible for calculating and returning feature rankings using Recursive Feature Elimination (RFE) with a Logistic Regression model.

```
def feat_importance_rfe(self, X, y):
    model = LogisticRegression()
    #Creates the RFE model
    rfe = RFE(model)
    rfe = rfe.fit(X, y)

    result_lg = pd.DataFrame()
    result_lg['Features'] = X.columns
    result_lg ['Ranking'] = rfe.ranking_
    result_lg.sort_values('Ranking', inplace=True , ascending = False)

    return result_lg
```

Let's break down how this method works:
1. Method Definition:

   def feat_importance_rfe(self, X, y): This is a method definition that takes three parameters: self, which is a reference to the instance of the class, X, which is a Pandas DataFrame containing the input features, and y, which is a NumPy array containing the target variable.
2. Creating a Logistic Regression Model:

   model = LogisticRegression(): An instance of the LogisticRegression classifier is created. Logistic Regression is used as the base model for feature ranking in the RFE process. The RFE technique aims to select the most important features by iteratively training the model with different subsets of features.
3. Creating the RFE Model:

rfe = RFE(model): An instance of the Recursive Feature Elimination (RFE) technique is created, with the LogisticRegression model as its base estimator. RFE is used to perform feature selection by recursively removing the least important features.

4. Fitting the RFE Model:

rfe = rfe.fit(X, y): The RFE model is fitted to the input features X and the target variable y. During this process, RFE iteratively trains the Logistic Regression model with different subsets of features and assigns rankings to each feature based on their importance.

5. Creating a Result DataFrame:

- result_lg = pd.DataFrame(): An empty Pandas DataFrame called result_lg is created to store the feature rankings.
- result_lg['Features'] = X.columns: A column named "Features" is added to the result_lg DataFrame, containing the names of the input features.
- result_lg['Ranking'] = rfe.ranking_: Another column named "Ranking" is added to the result_lg DataFrame, containing the feature rankings assigned by the RFE process. Lower rankings indicate more important features.

6. Sorting Feature Rankings:

result_lg.sort_values('Ranking', inplace=True, ascending=False): The result_lg DataFrame is sorted in descending order based on the "Ranking" column. This means that the features with lower rankings (more important) will appear at the top of the DataFrame.

7. Returning the Result DataFrame:

return result_lg: Finally, the method returns the result_lg DataFrame, which contains feature names and their corresponding rankings based on the RFE process.

The RFE technique is used for feature selection, and it helps identify the most important features for a given machine learning task. In this case, the rankings indicate the relative importance of each feature in making predictions using a Logistic Regression model.

Saving Prediction Result

In Process_Data class, the save_result() method in the code is responsible for saving the results of a prediction task into a CSV file. This method takes the actual target values (y_test), predicted values (y_pred), and a file name (fname) as input and then saves the results into a CSV file.

```
def save_result(self, y_test, y_pred, fname):
    # Convert y_test and y_pred to pandas Series for easier handling
    y_test_series = pd.Series(y_test)
    y_pred_series = pd.Series(y_pred)

    # Calculate y_result_series
```

```
y_result_series = pd.Series(y_pred - y_test == 0)
y_result_series = y_result_series.map({True: 'True', False: 'False'})

# Create a DataFrame to hold y_test, y_pred, and y_result
data = pd.DataFrame({'y_test': y_test_series, 'y_pred': y_pred_series, 'result': y_result_series})

# Save the DataFrame to a CSV file
data.to_csv(fname, index=False)
```

Here's a breakdown of how this method works:

1. Method Definition:

   def save_result(self, y_test, y_pred, fname): This is a method definition that takes four parameters: self, which refers to the instance of the class, y_test, which is a NumPy array or Pandas Series containing the actual target values, y_pred, which is a NumPy array or Pandas Series containing the predicted values, and fname, which is a string representing the file name for saving the results.

2. Converting to Pandas Series:

   - y_test_series = pd.Series(y_test): The y_test array is converted into a Pandas Series called y_test_series. This conversion makes it easier to manipulate and combine with other Series.

   - y_pred_series = pd.Series(y_pred): Similarly, the y_pred array is converted into a Pandas Series called y_pred_series.

3. Calculating the Result Series:

   - y_result_series = pd.Series(y_pred - y_test == 0): This line calculates a result series called y_result_series. It compares the predicted values (y_pred) with the actual values (y_test) element-wise and checks if they are equal. The result is a Boolean Series where True indicates that the prediction was correct, and False indicates an incorrect prediction.

   - y_result_series = y_result_series.map({True: 'True', False: 'False'}): The Boolean values in y_result_series are mapped to the strings 'True' and 'False', making it more human-readable.

4. Creating a DataFrame for Results:

   data = pd.DataFrame({'y_test': y_test_series, 'y_pred': y_pred_series, 'result': y_result_series}): A Pandas DataFrame called data is created to hold three columns: 'y_test' (containing actual target values), 'y_pred' (containing predicted values), and 'result' (containing 'True' or 'False' based on correctness of predictions). This DataFrame combines the actual and predicted values along with the result.

5. Saving the DataFrame to CSV:

   data.to_csv(fname, index=False): The data DataFrame is saved to a CSV file with the name specified by the fname parameter. The index=False argument ensures that the DataFrame index is not saved in the CSV file.

In summary, this method takes the actual and predicted values, computes whether each prediction was correct or not, and stores this information along with the original values in a CSV file for further analysis and reporting. This can be helpful for evaluating the performance of a machine learning model and comparing actual vs. predicted outcomes.

Helper_Plot Class

Create a new python file named helper_plot.py. Then, define a class named The Helper_Plot as utility class designed for plotting and visualizing data. It contains various methods and imports necessary libraries for creating visualizations.

```
#helper_plot.py
from tkinter import *
import seaborn as sns
import numpy as np
from pandastable import Table
from process_data import Process_Data
from sklearn.metrics import confusion_matrix, roc_curve, accuracy_score
from sklearn.model_selection import learning_curve

class Helper_Plot:
    def __init__(self):
        self.obj_data = Process_Data()
```

Let's go through the key aspects of this class:
1. Imports:
    - from tkinter import *: This import statement is used to import the necessary modules from the Tkinter library, which is commonly used for creating graphical user interfaces (GUIs) in Python.
    - import seaborn as sns: Seaborn is a data visualization library built on top of Matplotlib. It is often used to create visually appealing statistical graphics.
    - import numpy as np: NumPy is a library for numerical computations in Python.
    - from pandastable import Table: PandasTable is a library that provides a widget for displaying Pandas DataFrames in a Tkinter GUI.
2. Initialization:
    def __init__(self): The class constructor (__init__) initializes the Helper_Plot object. Inside the constructor, an instance of the Process_Data class (obj_data) is created. This suggests that the Helper_Plot class might work in conjunction with data processing methods from the Process_Data class.
3. Methods:
    The Helper_Plot class contains various methods for creating visualizations, such as plots, tables, and other graphical representations of data.

4. Integration with Process_Data:

The presence of an instance of the Process_Data class (obj_data) suggests that this class will work together with the data processing and preparation methods from the Process_Data class. It's common to have a separate utility class for plotting and visualization when working on data analysis and machine learning projects.

Overall, the Helper_Plot class serves as a utility for creating visualizations and working with data in a graphical form. It's used in conjunction with other classes and methods to analyze and visualize data for various data science and machine learning tasks.

Displaying Table

In Helper_Plot class, the shows_table() method in the code is responsible for displaying a Pandas DataFrame as a table in a new window created using Tkinter.

```python
def shows_table(self, root, df, width, height, title):
    frame = Toplevel(root) #new window
    self.table = Table(frame, dataframe=df, showtoolbar=True, showstatusbar=True)

    # Sets dimension of Toplevel
    frame.geometry(f"{width}x{height}")
    frame.title(title)
    self.table.show()
```

Let's break down how this method works:
1. Method Definition:

def shows_table(self, root, df, width, height, title): This is a method definition that takes five parameters:
   - self: This refers to the instance of the Helper_Plot class.
   - root: This is a reference to the Tkinter root window or parent window where the new window will be created.
   - df: This is the Pandas DataFrame that you want to display as a table.
   - width: This is an integer representing the width of the new window in pixels.
   - height: This is an integer representing the height of the new window in pixels.
   - title: This is a string representing the title of the new window.
2. Creating a New Window:

frame = Toplevel(root): This line creates a new Tkinter Toplevel window (frame) that will be used to display the table.
3. Creating the Table Widget:

self.table = Table(frame, dataframe=df, showtoolbar=True, showstatusbar=True): This line creates a PandasTable widget (self.table) within the new Toplevel window (frame).

It displays the DataFrame df as a table. The showtoolbar=True and showstatusbar=True arguments indicate that the table widget should include a toolbar and a status bar.

4. Setting the Window Dimensions and Title:
    - frame.geometry(f"{width}x{height}"): This line sets the dimensions (width and height) of the new window (frame) using the values provided in the width and height parameters.
    - frame.title(title): This line sets the title of the new window (frame) using the string provided in the title parameter.

5. Displaying the Table:
    self.table.show(): Finally, this line displays the table within the new window (frame).

In summary, the shows_table() method allows you to pop up a new window containing a table representation of a Pandas DataFrame. This can be useful for visualizing and exploring the data interactively within a GUI application built with Tkinter.

Modify Main_Class to Show Table of Dataset

The modified Main_Class in the code has been extended to include functionality related to data preprocessing and visualization using the Design_Window, Process_Data, and Helper_Plot classes. Let's break down the modifications and additions:

1. Import Statements:
    The code now includes import statements for the os module, indicating that it may interact with the file system.

2. Object Creation:
    Three new objects are created within the initialize() method:
    - self.obj_data = Process_Data(): An instance of the Process_Data class is created, indicating that this class will be used for data processing.
    - self.obj_plot = Helper_Plot(): An instance of the Helper_Plot class is created, suggesting that this class will be used for data visualization and plotting.

3. Data Preprocessing and Visualization:
    After creating instances of Process_Data and Helper_Plot, the code performs the following steps:
    - Reads the dataset using self.obj_data.preprocess().
    - Categorizes the dataset using self.obj_data.categorize(self.df).
    - Extracts input and output variables using self.obj_data.extract_cat_num_cols(self.df) and self.obj_data.extract_input_output_vars(self.df_final).

- Binds an event to self.obj_window.button1 to display the dataset as a table when the "LOAD DATASET" button is clicked.
4. Combo Box State:
   Initially, the code sets the state of self.obj_window.combo4 and self.obj_window.combo5 to 'disabled'. These combo boxes correspond to some functionality that is initially disabled until data splitting is done.

Overall, the modified Main_Class integrates data processing and visualization into the Tkinter-based GUI application. It uses the Process_Data class for data processing, the Helper_Plot class for visualization, and the Design_Window class for creating the GUI interface. The code performs data preprocessing tasks and binds events to interact with the GUI components. It provides an example of how to create a more comprehensive data science application using Tkinter and related classes.

```python
#main_class.py
import os
import tkinter as tk
from tkinter import *
from design_window import Design_Window
from process_data import Process_Data

class Main_Class:
    def __init__(self, root):
        self.initialize()

    def initialize(self):
        self.root = root
        width = 1500
        height = 750
        self.root.geometry(f"{width}x{height}")
        self.root.title("TKINTER AND DATA SCIENCE")

        #Creates necessary objects
        self.obj_window = Design_Window()
        self.obj_data = Process_Data()
        self.obj_plot = Helper_Plot()

        #Places widgets in root
        self.obj_window.add_widgets(self.root)

        #Reads dataset
        self.df = self.obj_data.preprocess()

        #Categorize dataset
        self.df_dummy = self.obj_data.categorize(self.df)

        #Extracts input and output variables
```

```
self.cat_cols, self.num_cols = self.obj_data.extract_cat_num_cols(self.df)
self.df_final = self.obj_data.encode_categorical_feats(self.df,
    self.cat_cols)
self.X, self.y = self.obj_data.extract_input_output_vars(self.df_final)

#Binds event
self.binds_event()

#Initially turns off combo4 and combo5 before data splitting is done
self.obj_window.combo4['state'] = 'disabled'
self.obj_window.combo5['state'] = 'disabled'

def binds_event(self):
    #Binds button1 to shows_table() function
    #Shows table if user clicks LOAD DATASET
    self.obj_window.button1.config(command = lambda:self.obj_plot.shows_table(self.root, self.df,
1400, 600, "Dataset"))

if __name__ == "__main__":
    root = tk.Tk()
    app = Main_Class(root)
    root.mainloop()
```

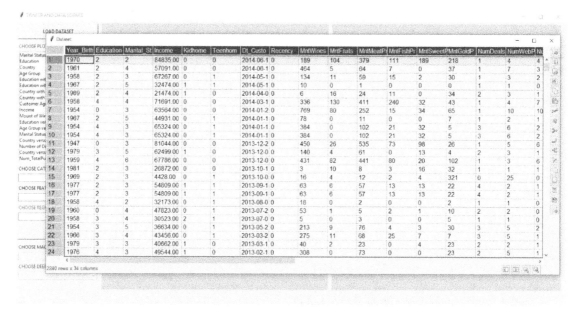

Figure 2 Showing the table of dataset

Run main_class.py script, then click on LOAD DATASET button to see the table of dataset as shown in figure 2

Plotting Pie Chart and Bar Chart

In Helper_Plot class, the plot_piechart() method defined in the code is responsible for creating a pie chart and a corresponding bar plot as subplots within a single Matplotlib figure.

```python
# Defines function to create pie chart and bar plot as subplots
def plot_piechart(self, df, var, figure, canvas, title=''):
    figure.clear()

    # Pie Chart (left subplot)
    plot1 = figure.add_subplot(2,1,1)
    label_list = list(df[var].value_counts().index)
    colors = sns.color_palette("deep", len(label_list))
    _, _, autopcts = plot1.pie(df[var].value_counts(), autopct="%1.1f%%", colors=colors,
        startangle=30, labels=label_list,
        wedgeprops={"linewidth": 2, "edgecolor": "white"},  # Add white edge
        shadow=True, textprops={'fontsize': 7})
    plot1.set_title("Distribution of " + var + " variable " + title, fontsize=10)

    # Bar Plot (right subplot)
    plot2 = figure.add_subplot(2,1,2)
    ax = df[var].value_counts().plot(kind="barh", color=colors, alpha=0.8, ax = plot2)
    for i, j in enumerate(df[var].value_counts().values):
        ax.text(.7, i, j, weight="bold", fontsize=7)

    plot2.set_title("Count of " + var + " cases " + title, fontsize=10)

    figure.tight_layout()
    canvas.draw()
```

Let's break down how this method works:

1. Method Definition:

    def plot_piechart(self, df, var, figure, canvas, title=''): This is a method definition that takes several parameters:

    - self: This refers to the instance of the class.
    - df: This is a Pandas DataFrame containing the data to be visualized.
    - var: This is a string representing the variable/column in the DataFrame that you want to visualize.
    - figure: This is a Matplotlib Figure object where the subplots will be created.
    - canvas: This is a Matplotlib FigureCanvasTkAgg object that will be used to draw the subplots.
    - title='': This is an optional string representing a title for the plots.

2. Clearing the Figure:

    figure.clear(): This line clears any previous content in the Matplotlib figure. It ensures that the new pie chart and bar plot will be drawn on a blank canvas.

3. Pie Chart (Left Subplot):
   - plot1 = figure.add_subplot(2,1,1): This line creates the left subplot for the pie chart within the figure. The add_subplot function is used to specify the subplot's position in a 2x1 grid (2 rows and 1 column of subplots).
   - The pie chart is created using Matplotlib's pie function. It displays the distribution of values in the specified column (var) of the DataFrame df. Various parameters are set to customize the pie chart, such as labels, colors, autopct (percentage labels), and more.
   - plot1.set_title("Distribution of " + var + " variable " + title, fontsize=10): This line sets the title for the pie chart subplot. The title includes the variable name (var) and an optional title provided as a parameter.

4. Bar Plot (Right Subplot):
   - plot2 = figure.add_subplot(2,1,2): This line creates the right subplot for the bar plot within the figure. Similar to the pie chart, it is positioned in the second row of the 2x1 grid.
   - The bar plot is created using Matplotlib's barh function. It displays the count of each unique value in the specified column (var) of the DataFrame df.
   - Labels and annotations are added to the bars to display the counts.
   - plot2.set_title("Count of " + var + " cases " + title, fontsize=10): This line sets the title for the bar plot subplot. The title includes the variable name (var) and an optional title provided as a parameter.

5. Tight Layout and Drawing:
   - figure.tight_layout(): This line ensures that the subplots are arranged neatly within the figure.
   - canvas.draw(): This line draws the subplots on the canvas, making them visible in the Matplotlib figure.

In summary, the plot_piechart() method allows you to create a pie chart and a bar plot as subplots within a Matplotlib figure, providing a visual representation of the distribution and counts of values in a specified DataFrame column. The optional title parameter allows you to add a title to the plots.

Pair of Histogram Plots

In Helper_Plot class, the another_versus_response() method defined in the code is responsible for creating a pair of histogram plots as subplots within a single Matplotlib figure. These histograms represent the distribution of a numerical feature (feat) for two different response classes (0 and 1, representing "Not Responsive" and "Responsive," respectively).

```
def another_versus_response(self, df, feat, num_bins, figure, canvas):
    figure.clear()
    plot1 = figure.add_subplot(2,1,1)

    colors = sns.color_palette("Set2")
    df[df['Response'] == 0][feat].plot(ax=plot1, kind='hist', bins=num_bins, edgecolor='black',
color=colors[0])
    plot1.set_title('Not Responsive', fontsize=15)
    plot1.set_xlabel(feat, fontsize=10)
    plot1.set_ylabel('Count', fontsize=10)
    data1 = []
    for p in plot1.patches:
        x = p.get_x() + p.get_width() / 2.
        y = p.get_height()
        plot1.annotate(format(y, '.0f'), (x, y), ha='center',
            va='center', xytext=(0, 10),
            weight="bold", fontsize=7, textcoords='offset points')
        data1.append([x, y])

    plot2 = figure.add_subplot(2,1,2)
    df[df['Response'] == 1][feat].plot(ax=plot2, kind='hist', bins=num_bins, edgecolor='black',
color=colors[1])
    plot2.set_title('Responsive', fontsize=15)
    plot2.set_xlabel(feat, fontsize=10)
    plot2.set_ylabel('Count', fontsize=10)
    data2 = []
    for p in plot2.patches:
        x = p.get_x() + p.get_width() / 2.
        y = p.get_height()
        plot2.annotate(format(y, '.0f'), (x, y), ha='center',
            va='center', xytext=(0, 10),
            weight="bold", fontsize=7, textcoords='offset points')
        data2.append([x, y])

    figure.tight_layout()
    canvas.draw()
```

Let's break down how this method works:
1. Method Definition:
   def another_versus_response(self, df, feat, num_bins, figure, canvas): This is a method definition that takes several parameters:
   - self: This refers to the instance of the class.

- df: This is a Pandas DataFrame containing the data to be visualized.
- feat: This is a string representing the numerical feature/column in the DataFrame that you want to visualize.
- num_bins: This is an integer specifying the number of bins or intervals for the histogram.
- figure: This is a Matplotlib Figure object where the subplots will be created.
- canvas: This is a Matplotlib FigureCanvasTkAgg object that will be used to draw the subplots.

2. Clearing the Figure:
   figure.clear(): This line clears any previous content in the Matplotlib figure. It ensures that the new histograms will be drawn on a blank canvas.
3. Histogram Plots for "Not Responsive" and "Responsive":
   - plot1 = figure.add_subplot(2,1,1): This line creates the upper subplot for the histogram representing the "Not Responsive" class within the figure. The add_subplot function is used to specify the subplot's position in a 2x1 grid (2 rows and 1 column of subplots).
   - colors = sns.color_palette("Set2"): This line defines a color palette (Set2) for the histograms.
   - df[df['Response'] == 0][feat].plot(ax=plot1, kind='hist', bins=num_bins, edgecolor='black', color=colors[0]): This line creates a histogram for the "Not Responsive" class. It filters the DataFrame to select only rows where Response is 0 and plots the histogram of the specified feature (feat) with the specified number of bins (num_bins). Customization options such as edge color and color are set.
   - The same steps are repeated to create a histogram for the "Responsive" class (Response is 1) in the lower subplot (plot2).
4. Customization:
   - Titles, x-axis labels, and y-axis labels are set for both subplots to provide context to the histograms.
   - Annotations are added to the top of each histogram bar to display the count of data points in each bin.
5. Tight Layout and Drawing:
   - figure.tight_layout(): This line ensures that the subplots are arranged neatly within the figure.
   - canvas.draw(): This line draws the subplots on the canvas, making them visible in the Matplotlib figure.

In summary, the another_versus_response() method allows you to create a pair of histogram plots within a Matplotlib figure. These histograms visualize the distribution of a specified numerical feature (feat) for two different response classes (0 and 1). The histograms provide insights into how the feature's distribution differs between the two classes.

Plotting Stacked Bar Chart

In Helper_Plot class, the put_label_stacked_bar() and dist_one_vs_another_plot() methods defined in the code are used to create a stacked bar chart for visualizing the relationship between two categorical variables.

The purpose of the code is to create a graphical user interface (GUI) application using Python's Tkinter library for data analysis and visualization in the context of data science. The application is designed to assist users in loading, exploring, and analyzing datasets, performing data preprocessing tasks, and generating various data visualizations.

```python
#Puts label inside stacked bar
def put_label_stacked_bar(self, ax,fontsize):
    #patches is everything inside of the chart
    for rect in ax.patches:
        # Find where everything is located
        height = rect.get_height()
        width = rect.get_width()
        x = rect.get_x()
        y = rect.get_y()

        # The height of the bar is the data value and can be used as the label
        label_text = f'{height:.0f}'

        # ax.text(x, y, text)
        label_x = x + width / 2
        label_y = y + height / 2

        # plots only when height is greater than specified value
        if height > 0:
            ax.text(label_x, label_y, label_text, \
                ha='center', va='center', \
                weight = "bold",fontsize=fontsize)

#Plots one variable against another variable
def dist_one_vs_another_plot(self, df, cat1, cat2, figure, canvas, title):
    figure.clear()
    plot1 = figure.add_subplot(1,1,1)

    group_by_stat = df.groupby([cat1, cat2]).size()
    colors = sns.color_palette("Set2", len(df[cat1].unique()))
    stacked_data = group_by_stat.unstack()
    group_by_stat.unstack().plot(kind='bar', stacked=True, ax=plot1, grid=True, color=colors)
```

```
plot1.set_title(title, fontsize=12)
plot1.set_ylabel('Number of Cases', fontsize=10)
plot1.set_xlabel(cat1, fontsize=10)
self.put_label_stacked_bar(plot1,7)
# Set font for tick labels
plot1.tick_params(axis='both', which='major', labelsize=8)
plot1.tick_params(axis='both', which='minor', labelsize=8)
plot1.legend(fontsize=8)
figure.tight_layout()
canvas.draw()
```

Let's break down how these methods work:

1. put_label_stacked_bar Method:

    This method is responsible for adding labels inside each bar of a stacked bar chart.

    - ax: This parameter represents the Axes object (subplot) where the stacked bar chart is plotted.
    - fontsize: This parameter specifies the font size for the labels.

2. Here's how the method works:

    - It iterates through each bar (rectangle) in the stacked bar chart.
    - For each bar, it retrieves information about its position, height, width, and coordinates.
    - The height of the bar (data value) is used as the label text.
    - The label's position (label_x and label_y) is calculated as the center of the bar.
    - Labels are placed inside the bars only if the bar's height is greater than a specified value (ensuring that small bars don't get cluttered with labels).

3. dist_one_vs_another_plot() Method:

    This method creates a stacked bar chart to visualize the distribution of one categorical variable against another categorical variable. The chart represents the number of cases for each combination of the two categorical variables.

    - df: This parameter is a Pandas DataFrame containing the data to be visualized.
    - cat1: This parameter is a string representing the first categorical variable.
    - cat2: This parameter is a string representing the second categorical variable.
    - figure: This parameter is a Matplotlib Figure object where the stacked bar chart will be created.
    - canvas: This parameter is a Matplotlib FigureCanvasTkAgg object used to draw the chart.
    - title: This parameter is a string specifying the title of the chart.

4. Here's how the method works:

    - It first clears any previous content in the Matplotlib figure.
    - It creates a single subplot within the figure (plot1) to display the stacked bar chart.

- The data is grouped by the two categorical variables (cat1 and cat2), and the size of each group is calculated.
- Colors are defined for each category in cat1.
- The data is then unstacked, and a stacked bar chart is created with bars representing the number of cases for each combination of cat1 and cat2.
- Labels are added inside each bar using the put_label_stacked_bar method.
- The chart is customized with titles, axis labels, legend, grid, and tick label fonts.
- Finally, the chart is drawn on the canvas and ensures that the subplots are arranged neatly within the figure.

In summary, these methods help you visualize the distribution and relationships between categorical variables using stacked bar charts, and they ensure that labels are placed inside the bars for better readability.

Box Plot Visualization

In Helper_Plot class, the box_plot() method is designed to create a box plot visualization of the dataset, showing the distribution of a numerical variable (y) for different categories or groups specified by two categorical variables (x and hue). This type of plot is useful for visualizing the distribution of a numerical variable across different categories and identifying any potential outliers or variations within each category.

```
def box_plot(self, df, x, y, hue, figure, canvas, title):
    figure.clear()
    plot1 = figure.add_subplot(1,1,1)

    #Creates boxplot of Num_TotalPurchases versus Num_Dependants
    sns.boxplot(data = df, x = x, y = y, hue = hue, ax=plot1)
    plot1.set_title(title, fontsize=14)
    plot1.set_xlabel(x, fontsize=10)
    plot1.set_ylabel(y, fontsize=10)
    figure.tight_layout()
    canvas.draw()
```

Here's an explanation of the method's parameters and functionality:
- df: The dataset (DataFrame) containing the data to be visualized.
- x: The name of the first categorical variable, which determines the groups or categories along the x-axis of the box plot.
- y: The name of the numerical variable whose distribution will be visualized using the box plot. The distribution of this variable will be represented using boxes and whiskers.
- hue: The name of the second categorical variable (optional). If specified, it determines the color-coding of the box plot, allowing you to differentiate between groups within the

primary categories defined by x. This is useful when you want to visualize a third categorical dimension.

- figure: The Matplotlib figure object where the box plot will be created. The figure object should be cleared before creating the new box plot to avoid overlapping with previous visualizations.
- canvas: The Matplotlib canvas associated with the figure. This canvas is used to display the updated plot.
- title: The title for the box plot, which is displayed above the visualization.

The main steps and functionality of the box_plot method are as follows:
1. It clears any existing content in the Matplotlib figure to prepare it for the new box plot.
2. It creates a subplot within the figure using figure.add_subplot(1, 1, 1).
3. It uses Seaborn's sns.boxplot function to generate the box plot. The box plot displays the distribution of the y variable for each category defined by x and, if specified, further differentiated by hue.
4. It sets the title, x-axis label, and y-axis label for the box plot based on the provided parameters (title, x, and y).
5. Finally, it tightens the layout of the plot within the figure, ensuring that the plot elements do not overlap, and then updates the canvas to display the new box plot.

In summary, the box_plot() method allows users to visualize the distribution of a numerical variable across different categories or groups defined by one or two categorical variables. The resulting box plot provides insights into the central tendency, spread, and potential outliers of the data within each category, making it a valuable tool for exploratory data analysis.

Distribution of Marital Status

In Helper_Plot class, the choose_plot() method focuses on choosing and displaying a specific type of plot based on the user's selection (chosen) from a dropdown or input.

```
def choose_plot(self, df1, df2, chosen, figure1, canvas1, figure2, canvas2):
    print(chosen)
    if chosen == "Marital Status":
        self.plot_piechart(df2, "Marital_Status", figure1, canvas1)
```

Here's an explanation of the method's parameters and functionality:
- df1 and df2: These are DataFrames representing different subsets of the data. It's that df2 is a modified or categorized version of df1, which may be used for specific types of visualizations.

- chosen: This parameter represents the user's choice or selection, typically from a dropdown or input widget. It determines which type of plot to generate based on the user's selection.
- figure1 and canvas1: These are Matplotlib figure and canvas objects where the first type of plot will be created and displayed.
- figure2 and canvas2: Similar to figure1 and canvas1, these objects are used for a different type of plot that may be displayed alongside the first plot.

Here's what this code does:
1. It checks the value of the chosen parameter to determine if it matches a specific option, in this case, "Marital Status."
2. If the user has selected "Marital Status," it calls the plot_piechart() method with specific arguments:
   - df2: This DataFrame contains data related to marital status.
   - "Marital_Status": This is the name of the variable (column) within df2 that will be used to create the pie chart.
   - figure1 and canvas1: These are the Matplotlib figure and canvas objects where the pie chart will be displayed.
3. The plot_piechart() method is expected to create and display a pie chart showing the distribution of marital status based on the data in df2.

In summary, the choose_plot() method is responsible for determining the type of plot to display based on the user's selection (chosen). If the user chooses "Marital Status," it triggers the creation of a pie chart showing the distribution of marital status using data from df2. This approach allows for dynamic plot generation based on user input.

Then, modify Main_Class class as follows:

```python
#main_class.py
import os
import tkinter as tk
from tkinter import *
from design_window import Design_Window
from process_data import Process_Data
from helper_plot import Helper_Plot

class Main_Class:
    def __init__(self, root):
        self.initialize()

    def initialize(self):
        self.root = root
        width = 1500
```

```
        height = 750
        self.root.geometry(f"{width}x{height}")
        self.root.title("TKINTER AND DATA SCIENCE")

        #Creates necessary objects
        self.obj_window = Design_Window()
        self.obj_data = Process_Data()
        self.obj_plot = Helper_Plot()

        #Places widgets in root
        self.obj_window.add_widgets(self.root)

        #Reads dataset
        self.df = self.obj_data.preprocess()

        #Categorize dataset
        self.df_dummy = self.obj_data.categorize(self.df)

        #Extracts input and output variables
        self.cat_cols, self.num_cols = self.obj_data.extract_cat_num_cols(self.df)
        self.df_final = self.obj_data.encode_categorical_feats(self.df, self.cat_cols)
        self.X, self.y = self.obj_data.extract_input_output_vars(self.df_final)

        #Binds event
        self.binds_event()

        #Initially turns off combo4 and combo5 before data splitting is done
        self.obj_window.combo4['state'] = 'disabled'
        self.obj_window.combo5['state'] = 'disabled'

    def binds_event(self):
        #Binds button1 to shows_table() function
        #Shows table if user clicks LOAD DATASET
        self.obj_window.button1.config(command = lambda:self.obj_plot.shows_table(self.root, self.df,
1400, 600, "Dataset"))

        #Binds listbox to a function
        self.obj_window.listbox.bind("<<ListboxSelect>>", self.choose_list_widget)

    def choose_list_widget(self, event):
        chosen = self.obj_window.listbox.get(self.obj_window.listbox.curselection())
        print(chosen)
        self.obj_plot.choose_plot(self.df, self.df_dummy, chosen,
            self.obj_window.figure1, self.obj_window.canvas1,
            self.obj_window.figure2, self.obj_window.canvas2)

if __name__ == "__main__":
    root = tk.Tk()
    app = Main_Class(root)
    root.mainloop()
```

This line of code is binding an event handler function to the <<ListboxSelect>> event of a Listbox widget.

```
#Binds listbox to a function
self.obj_window.listbox.bind("<<ListboxSelect>>", self.choose_list_widget)
```

Here's what it does:
1. self.obj_window.listbox: This refers to a Listbox widget created in the obj_window object (an instance of the Design_Window class).
2. .bind("<<ListboxSelect>>", self.choose_list_widget): This is the binding statement.
3. "<<ListboxSelect>>": This is the event to which the function is being bound. It's the event that gets triggered when an item in the Listbox is selected.
4. self.choose_list_widget: This is the function (event handler) that will be executed when the <<ListboxSelect>> event occurs. In this case, it's choose_list_widget, which is a method of the Main_Class class.

When a user selects an item in the Listbox by clicking on it, the <<ListboxSelect>> event is triggered. When this event occurs, the choose_list_widget method (self.choose_list_widget) will be executed. This allows you to define specific actions or behavior that should occur when the user selects an item from the Listbox.

Then, in Main_Class, add a new method named choose_list_widget(). It is an event handler that is executed when the <<ListboxSelect>> event occurs, which happens when a user selects an item in the Listbox widget.

```
def choose_list_widget(self, event):
    chosen = self.obj_window.listbox.get(self.obj_window.listbox.curselection())
    print(chosen)
    self.obj_plot.choose_plot(self.df, self.df_dummy, chosen,
        self.obj_window.figure1, self.obj_window.canvas1,
        self.obj_window.figure2, self.obj_window.canvas2)
```

Here's a breakdown of what this function does:
1. chosen = self.obj_window.listbox.get(self.obj_window.listbox.curselection()): This line retrieves the currently selected item(s) from the Listbox widget (self.obj_window.listbox) using the curselection() method. It assigns the selected item(s) to the chosen variable. Since Listboxes can support multiple selections (if configured as such), chosen will contain a list of selected items.
2. print(chosen): This line simply prints the selected item(s) to the console. This is for debugging or informational purposes and helps you see what the user has selected.

3. self.obj_plot.choose_plot(...): This line calls the choose_plot() method of the self.obj_plot object (an instance of the Helper_Plot class). It passes several arguments to this method:
4. self.df: This is the main DataFrame containing your data.
5. self.df_dummy: This is another DataFrame, a modified version of the main DataFrame, used for visualization purposes.
6. chosen: This is the item selected in the Listbox, representing the user's choice.
7. self.obj_window.figure1 and self.obj_window.canvas1: These are objects used for displaying a plot in the user interface.
8. self.obj_window.figure2 and self.obj_window.canvas2: These are additional objects used for displaying plots.

Based on the selected item (chosen), the choose_plot() method generates and displays a specific type of data visualization using the provided data and UI elements.

In summary, the choose_list_widget() function serves as a bridge between the user's selection in the Listbox and the generation of specific data visualizations in your application. It allows the user to interactively choose what type of visualization they want to see.

Then, run main_class.py. Select Marital Status in list widget to see the distribution of marital status in the dataset as shown in figure 3.

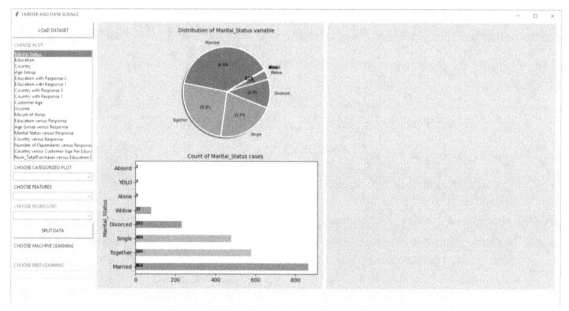

Figure 3 The distribution of marital status

Distribution of Education

Add this code to the end of choose_plot() method in Helper_Plot class. When the user selects "Education" in the Listbox (chosen == "Education"), the self.obj_plot.choose_plot() method is called with specific arguments to generate and display a pie chart related to the "Education" feature.

```
elif chosen == "Education":
    self.plot_piechart(df2, "Education", figure2, canvas2)
```

The choose_plot() method, based on the value of chosen (which is "Education" in this case), will generate a specific type of data visualization (in this case, a pie chart) using the provided data (from self.df and self.df_dummy) and display it within the UI elements (self.obj_window.figure2 and self.obj_window.canvas2).

Then, run main_class.py. Select Education in list widget to see the distribution of education in the dataset as shown in figure 4.

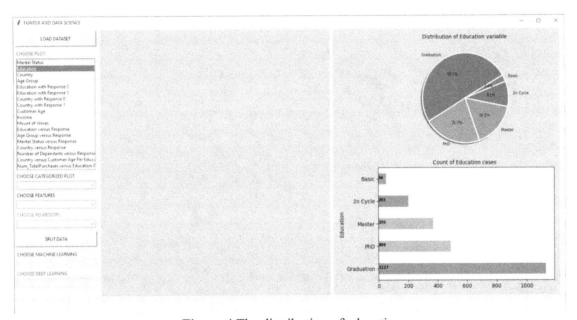

Figure 4 The distribution of education

Distribution of Country

Add this code to the end of choose_plot() method in Helper_Plot class:

```
elif chosen == "Country":
    self.plot_piechart(df2, "Country", figure1, canvas1)
```

When the user selects "Country" from the Listbox, a specific data visualization is generated and displayed within user interface. This functionality is achieved through the choose_list_widget() function, which is bound to the Listbox's selection event. When "Country" is selected, it triggers the choose_plot() method of the self.obj_plot object, an instance of the Helper_Plot class. This method takes several arguments, including the main data DataFrame (self.df), a modified DataFrame for visualization (self.df_dummy), and the specific selection made by the user ("Country"). Additionally, it uses UI elements (self.obj_window.figure1 and self.obj_window.canvas1) to display the resulting visualization.

The choose_plot() method, depending on the value of the selection ("Country" in this case), dynamically generates a pie chart based on the data provided in self.df and self.df_dummy. This allows your application to respond to user interactions, enabling users to explore different aspects of the dataset visually. By binding the function to the Listbox selection event, your application enhances user interactivity and facilitates the exploration of data categories through intuitive data visualizations, making it more user-friendly and engaging.

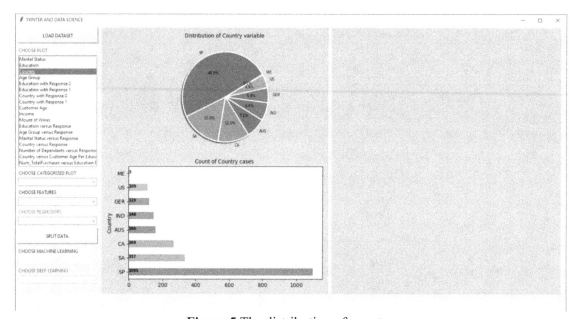

Figure 5 The distribution of country

Distribution of Age Group

Add this code to the end of choose_plot() method in Helper_Plot class:

```
elif chosen == "Age Group":
    self.plot_piechart(df2, "AgeGroup", figure2, canvas2)
```

In this code, when the user selects "Age Group" from the Listbox, it triggers the execution of the choose_list_widget() function. Within this function, there's a conditional branch that checks if the chosen option is "Age Group." If this condition is met, it calls the plot_piechart() method of the self.obj_plot object, passing the modified DataFrame df2, specifically the "AgeGroup" column, as well as UI elements (figure2 and canvas2). As a result, when "Age Group" is selected, it dynamically generates a pie chart based on the distribution of age groups in the dataset, providing users with a visual representation of age group demographics within the data, as shown in figure 6. This interactive feature enhances the user experience by allowing users to explore and understand data patterns through intuitive data visualizations.

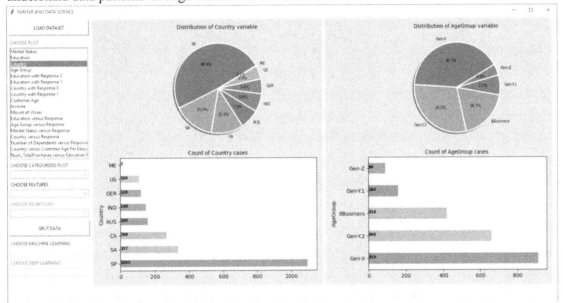

Figure 6 The distribution of age group

Distribution of Education with Response 0

Add this code to the end of choose_plot() method in Helper_Plot class:

```
elif chosen == "Education with Response 0":
    self.plot_piechart(df2[df2.Response==0], "Education", figure1, canvas1, " with Response 0")
```

In this code, when the user selects "Education with Response 0" from the Listbox, it triggers the execution of the choose_list_widget() function. Within this function, there's a conditional branch that checks if the chosen option is "Education with Response 0." If this condition is met, it filters the DataFrame df2 to include only rows where the "Response" column equals 0 (indicating non-responsiveness), and then calls the plot_piechart() method of the self.obj_plot object. It passes the filtered DataFrame, specifically the "Education" column, along with UI elements (figure1 and canvas1), and an additional title extension " with Response 0." As a result, when "Education with Response 0" is selected, it dynamically generates a pie chart representing the distribution of education levels among non-responsive customers, allowing users to visually explore the educational background of unresponsive customers in the dataset. This interactive feature aids in analyzing the characteristics of customers who did not respond to marketing efforts as shown in figure 7.

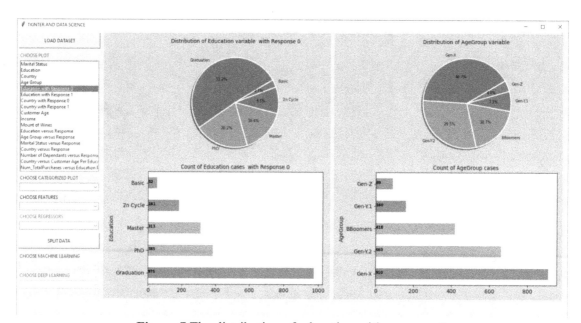

Figure 7 The distribution of education with response 0

Distribution of Education with Response 1

Add this code to the end of choose_plot() method in Helper_Plot class:

```
elif chosen == "Education with Response 1":
    self.plot_piechart(df2[df2.Response==1], "Education", figure2, canvas2, " with Response 1")
```

In this code, when the user selects "Education with Response 1" from the Listbox, it triggers the execution of the choose_list_widget() function. Within this function, there's a conditional branch that checks if the chosen option is "Education with Response 1." If this condition is met, it filters the DataFrame df2 to include only rows where the "Response" column equals 1 (indicating responsiveness), and then calls the plot_piechart() method of the self.obj_plot object. It passes the filtered DataFrame, specifically the "Education" column, along with UI elements (figure2 and canvas2), and an additional title extension " with Response 1." As a result, when "Education with

Response 1" is selected, it dynamically generates a pie chart representing the distribution of education levels among responsive customers, allowing users to visually explore the educational background of responsive customers in the dataset. This interactive feature aids in analyzing the characteristics of customers who responded positively to marketing efforts, as shown in figure 8.

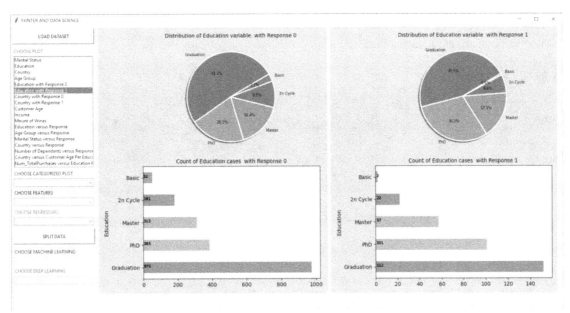

Figure 8 The distribution of education with response 1

Distribution of Country with Response 0 and 1

Add this code to the end of choose_plot() method in Helper_Plot class:

```
elif chosen == "Country with Response 0":
    self.plot_piechart(df2[df2.Response==0], "Country", figure1, canvas1, " with Response 0")

elif chosen == "Country with Response 1":
    self.plot_piechart(df2[df2.Response==1], "Country", figure2, canvas2, " with Response 1")
```

In this code, when the user selects either "Country with Response 0" or "Country with Response 1" from the Listbox, it triggers the execution of the choose_list_widget() function. Within this function, there are conditional branches that check the chosen option. If the chosen option is "Country with Response 0," it filters the DataFrame df2 to include only rows where the "Response" column equals 0 (indicating non-responsiveness). It then calls the plot_piechart() method of the self.obj_plot object, passing the filtered DataFrame, specifically the "Country" column, along with UI elements (figure1 and canvas1), and an additional title extension " with

Response 0." This generates a pie chart showing the distribution of countries among non-responsive customers. Similarly, if the chosen option is "Country with Response 1," it filters the DataFrame to include only rows where the "Response" column equals 1 (indicating responsiveness), and then generates a pie chart for the distribution of countries among responsive customers using UI elements (figure2 and canvas2) and an additional title extension " with Response 1." These features enable users to visually explore the impact of a customer's country of residence on their responsiveness to marketing efforts, providing valuable insights for marketing strategies. The result is shown in figure 9.

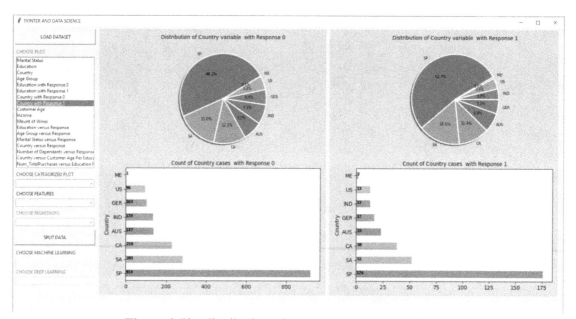

Figure 9 The distribution of country with response 0 or 1

Histogram of Income

Add this code to the end of choose_plot() method in Helper_Plot class:

```
elif chosen == "Income":
    self.another_versus_response(df1, "Income", 32, figure1, canvas1)
```

In this code segment, when the user selects "Income" from the Listbox, it triggers the execution of the choose_list_widget() function. Within this function, there is a conditional branch that checks if the chosen option is "Income." If it is, the code calls the another_versus_response() method, passing the DataFrame df1, the feature "Income," the number of bins (set to 32), UI elements (figure1 and canvas1), and an empty title. This method generates a subplot with two histograms. The first histogram shows the distribution of income for non-responsive customers (those with "Response" equal to 0), and the second histogram shows the distribution of income for responsive customers (those with "Response" equal to 1). By comparing these histograms, users can gain insights into how income levels may impact customer responsiveness to marketing efforts. The result is shown in figure 10.

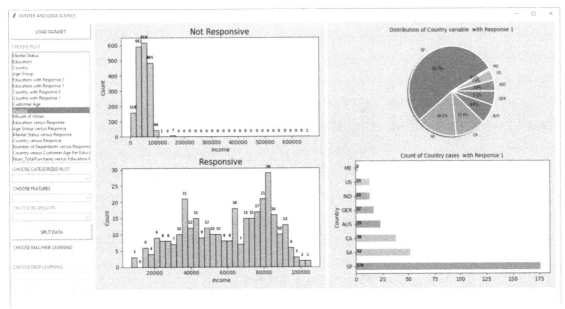

Figure 10 The histogram of income

Histogram of Customer Age

Add this code to the end of choose_plot() method in Helper_Plot class:

```
elif chosen == "Customer Age":
    self.another_versus_response(df1, "Customer_Age", 32, figure1, canvas1)
```

In this code, when the user selects "Customer Age" from the Listbox, it triggers the execution of the choose_list_widget() function. Within this function, there is a conditional branch that checks if the chosen option is "Customer Age." If it is, the code calls the another_versus_response() method, passing the DataFrame df1, the feature "Customer_Age," the number of bins (set to 32), UI elements (figure1 and canvas1), and an empty title. This method generates a subplot with two histograms. The first histogram shows the distribution of customer age for non-responsive customers (those with "Response" equal to 0), and the second histogram shows the distribution of customer age for responsive customers (those with "Response" equal to 1). By comparing these histograms, users can gain insights into how customer age may impact customer responsiveness to marketing efforts. The result is shown in figure 11.

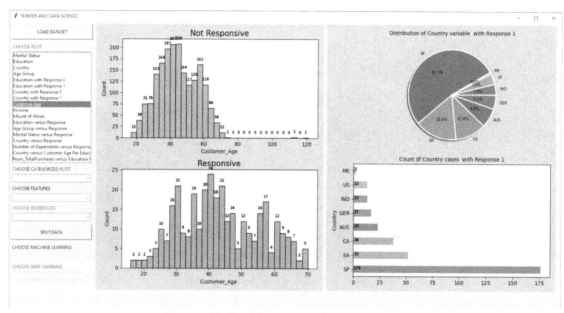

Figure 11 The histogram of customer age

Histogram of Amount of Purchased Wines

Add this code to the end of choose_plot() method in Helper_Plot class:

```
elif chosen == "Amount of Wines":
    self.another_versus_response(df1, "MntWines", 32, figure2, canvas2)
```

In this code, when the user selects "Amount of Wines" from the Listbox, it triggers the execution of the choose_list_widget() function. Within this function, there is a conditional branch that checks if the chosen option is "Mount of Wines." If it is, the code calls the another_versus_response() method, passing the DataFrame df1, the feature "MntWines," the number of bins (set to 32), UI elements (figure2 and canvas2), and an empty title. This method generates a subplot with two histograms. The first histogram shows the distribution of the amount of wines purchased by non-responsive customers (those with "Response" equal to 0), and the second histogram shows the distribution of the amount of wines purchased by responsive customers (those with "Response" equal to 1). By comparing these histograms, users can gain insights into how the amount of wines purchased may impact customer responsiveness to marketing efforts. The result is shown in figure 12.

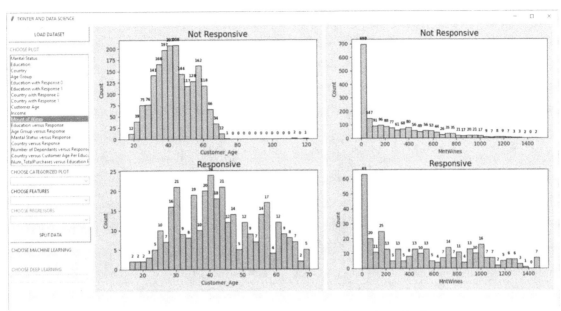

Figure 12 The histogram of amount of purchased wines

Distribution of Education versus Response

Add this code to the end of choose_plot() method in Helper_Plot class:

```
elif chosen == "Education versus Response":
    self.dist_one_vs_another_plot(df2, "Education", "Response", figure2, canvas2, chosen)
```

In this code, when the user selects "Education versus Response" from the Listbox, it triggers the execution of the choose_list_widget() function. Within this function, there is a conditional branch that checks if the chosen option is "Education versus Response." If it is, the code calls the dist_one_vs_another_plot() method, passing the DataFrame df2, the features "Education" and "Response," UI elements (figure2 and canvas2), and the title "Education versus Response." This method generates a stacked bar plot that visualizes the relationship between a customer's education level (e.g., high school, university degree) and their responsiveness to marketing efforts (0 or 1). Each bar in the plot represents a specific education category, and the height of each segment within the bar indicates the count of responsive and non-responsive customers within that education category. This visualization helps users understand how education level might influence customer responsiveness. The result is shown in figure 13.

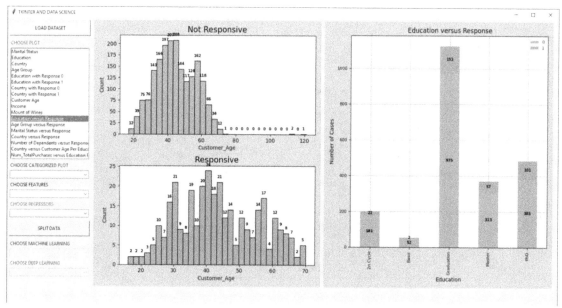

Figure 13 The distribution of education versus response

Distribution of Age Group versus Response

Add this code to the end of choose_plot() method in Helper_Plot class:

```
elif chosen == "Age Group versus Response":
    self.dist_one_vs_another_plot(df2, "AgeGroup", "Response", figure1, canvas1, chosen)
```

The purpose of this code is to create a stacked bar plot that visually represents the relationship between different age groups of customers and their responsiveness to marketing efforts. Specifically, it focuses on comparing how different age groups within the dataset respond to marketing campaigns.

Here's how it works:
1. chosen is a variable that holds the currently selected item from the Listbox in the graphical user interface (GUI).
2. When the user selects "Age Group versus Response" from the Listbox, this condition (elif chosen == "Age Group versus Response") is met, and the code block is executed.
3. The dist_one_vs_another_plot() method is called with specific parameters:
    df2 is the DataFrame containing the dataset, which includes columns for "AgeGroup" (categorized age groups) and "Response" (indicating whether a customer responded to marketing).
    * "AgeGroup" and "Response" are specified as the two variables to be analyzed in the plot.

- figure1 and canvas1 are UI elements used for displaying the plot.
- "Age Group versus Response" is provided as the title of the plot.

The resulting plot will visually represent how each age group (e.g., Generation X, Baby Boomers) is divided into segments, with each segment representing the count of customers who responded (1) and those who did not respond (0) to marketing efforts. This visualization helps marketers and data analysts understand the responsiveness of different age groups and make data-driven decisions related to marketing strategies and targeting specific customer demographics. The result is shown in figure 14.

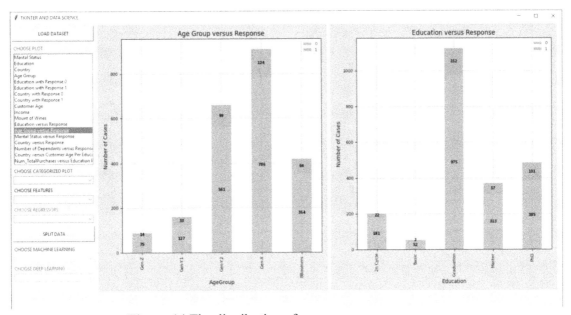

Figure 14 The distribution of age group versus response

Distribution of Marital Status versus Response

Add this code to the end of choose_plot() method in Helper_Plot class:

```
elif chosen == "Marital Status versus Response":
    self.dist_one_vs_another_plot(df2, "Marital_Status", "Response", figure2, canvas2, chosen)
```

The purpose of this code is to create a stacked bar plot that visually represents the relationship between different marital statuses of customers and their responsiveness to marketing efforts. Specifically, it focuses on comparing how different marital statuses within the dataset influence the response of customers to marketing campaigns.

The resulting plot will visually represent how each marital status category (e.g., Married, Single, Divorced) is divided into segments, with each segment representing the count of customers who responded (1) and those who did not respond (0) to marketing efforts. This visualization helps marketers and data analysts understand the impact of marital status on customer responsiveness, aiding in marketing strategy decisions and targeted campaigns. The result is shown in figure 15.

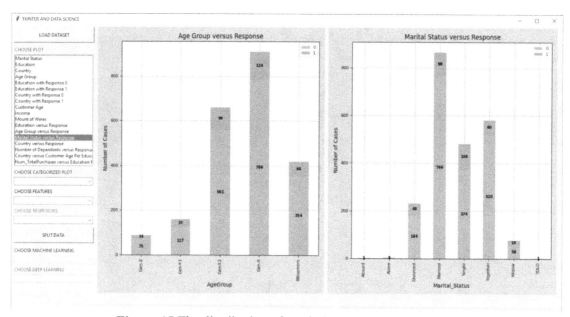

Figure 15 The distribution of marital status versus response

Distribution of Country versus Response

Add this code to the end of choose_plot() method in Helper_Plot class:

```
elif chosen == "Country versus Response":
    self.dist_one_vs_another_plot(df2, "Country", "Response", figure1, canvas1, chosen)
```

The purpose of this code block is to create a stacked bar plot that visually represents the relationship between different countries of customers and their responsiveness to marketing efforts. Specifically, it focuses on comparing how different countries within the dataset influence the response of customers to marketing campaigns.

The resulting plot will visually represent how each country category (e.g., Spain, France, Germany) is divided into segments, with each segment representing the count of customers who responded (1) and those who did not respond (0) to marketing efforts. This visualization helps marketers and data analysts understand the impact of the country of residence on customer responsiveness, aiding in marketing strategy decisions and targeted campaigns. The result is shown in figure 16.

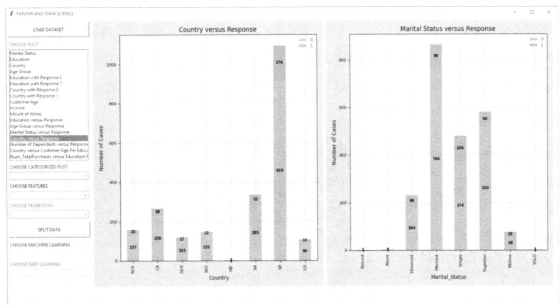

Figure 16 The distribution of country versus response

Distribution of Number of Dependants versus Response

Add this code to the end of choose_plot() method in Helper_Plot class:

```
elif chosen == "Number of Dependants versus Response":
    self.dist_one_vs_another_plot(df2, "Num_Dependants", "Response", figure2, canvas2, chosen)
```

The resulting plot will visually represent how the count of dependants in a customer's household impacts their responsiveness to marketing efforts. It will show stacked bars, with each segment representing the count of customers who responded (1) and those who did not respond (0) based on the number of dependants. This visualization can help marketers and analysts understand the family structure's role in customer responses and guide marketing strategies accordingly. The result is shown in figure 17.

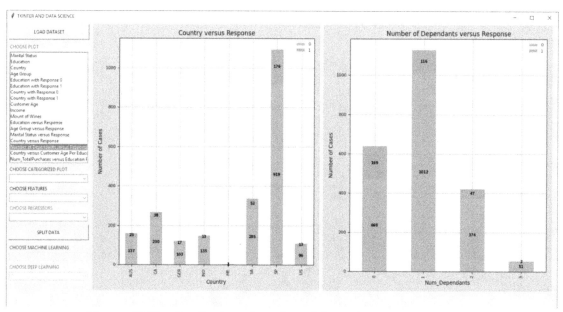

Figure 17 The distribution of number of dependants versus response

Distribution of Customer Ages Among Different Educational Levels and Countries

Add this code to the end of choose_plot() method in Helper_Plot class:

```
elif chosen == "Country versus Customer Age Per Education":
    self.box_plot(df1, "Country", "Customer_Age", "Education", figure1, canvas1, chosen)
```

The code serves the purpose of generating a box plot to visualize how customer ages are distributed among different education levels and countries. This code is designed to analyze and represent the variations in customer ages within specific educational groups and across various countries.

When a user selects "Country versus Customer Age Per Education" from the Listbox in the graphical user interface (GUI), the associated condition is met, triggering the execution of this code. The box_plot() function is then called with specific parameters. It takes as input a DataFrame (df1) that contains the dataset, including columns for "Country," "Customer_Age" (representing customer ages), and "Education" (indicating the educational background of customers). The "Country" variable is specified as the x-axis, "Customer_Age" as the y-axis, and "Education" as the hue variable for color categorization. Additionally, it utilizes figure1 and canvas1 as UI elements for displaying the resulting plot, with the title "Country versus Customer Age Per Education."

The generated box plot will display multiple boxes, each corresponding to a unique combination of country and education level. These boxes visually represent the distribution of customer ages within these specific groups. Analyzing this plot can provide valuable insights into age variations among customers from different countries and educational backgrounds. Such insights can be instrumental in tailoring marketing strategies or targeted campaigns to effectively reach and engage specific customer segments. The result is shown in figure 18.

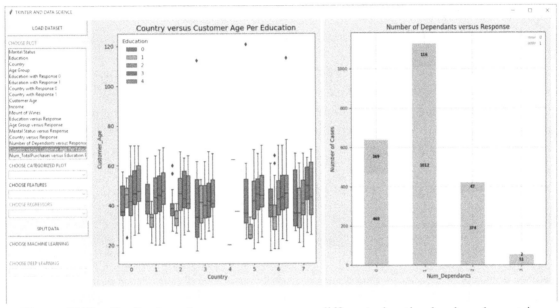

Figure 18 The distribution of customer ages among different education levels and countries

Distribution of Total Number of Purchases and Educational Levels within Different Marital Status

Add this code to the end of choose_plot() method in Helper_Plot class:

```
elif chosen == "Num_TotalPurchases versus Education Per Marital Status":
    self.box_plot(df1, "Education", "Num_TotalPurchases", "Marital_Status", figure2, canvas2, chosen)
```

The code is responsible for creating a box plot that illustrates the relationship between the total number of purchases made by customers ("Num_TotalPurchases") and their educational levels ("Education") within different marital status categories ("Marital_Status"). This visualization is useful for understanding how the number of purchases varies among customers with different educational backgrounds across various marital status groups.

When a user selects "Num_TotalPurchases versus Education Per Marital Status" from the Listbox in the graphical user interface (GUI), the associated condition is satisfied, and this code is executed. The box_plot() function is then invoked with specific parameters. It takes a DataFrame (df1) containing the dataset as input, including columns for "Education," "Num_TotalPurchases," and "Marital_Status." In the resulting box plot, "Education" is designated as the x-axis variable, "Num_TotalPurchases" as the y-axis variable, and "Marital_Status" as the hue variable for distinguishing different marital status categories. Furthermore, it utilizes figure2 and canvas2 as UI components for presenting the generated plot, along with the title "Num_TotalPurchases versus Education Per Marital Status."

The resulting box plot will display a series of boxes, each representing a specific combination of education level and marital status. These boxes visually depict the distribution of the total number of purchases made by customers within these distinct groups. Analyzing this plot can provide insights into how customers' educational backgrounds and marital statuses relate to their purchasing behaviors. Such insights can be valuable for tailoring marketing strategies or product offerings to different customer segments, optimizing business operations, and making data-driven decisions. The result is shown in figure 19.

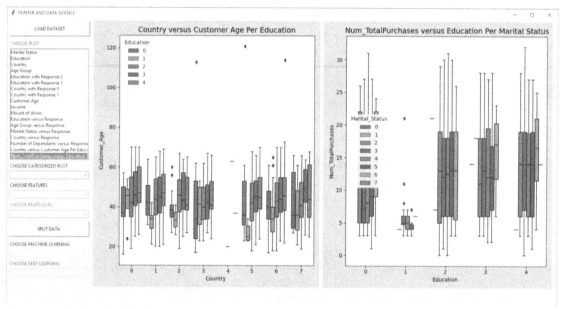

Figure 19 The distribution of total number of purchases and educational levels within different marital status

Distribution of Categorized Income versus Response

Add this code to the end of binds_event() method in Main_Class:

```
#Binds listbox to a function
self.obj_window.listbox.bind("<<ListboxSelect>>", self.choose_list_widget)
```

This code binds a function to the <<ComboboxSelected>> event of a tkinter Combobox widget (self.obj_window.combo1). The purpose of this code is to associate a specific action or behavior with the selection of an item from combo1.

When the user selects an item from combo1, the choose_combobox1() function will be triggered. This function will be responsible for handling the user's choice and performing the associated actions or displaying relevant information based on the selected item.

Binding events to widgets like this is a common practice in GUI applications to make the interface responsive and interactive. In this specific case, it suggests that the code is designed to react dynamically to the user's selection from the combo box, enhancing the user experience and allowing for more versatile interactions with the application.

Then, define a new method named choose_combobox1() in Main_Class:

```
def choose_combobox1(self, event):
    chosen = self.obj_window.combo1.get()
    self.obj_plot.choose_category(self.df_dummy, chosen,
        self.obj_window.figure1, self.obj_window.canvas1,
        self.obj_window.figure2, self.obj_window.canvas2)
```

This code defines the choose_combobox1() function, which is triggered when an item is selected in the combo1 tkinter Combobox widget.

Here's a breakdown of what this function does:
1. chosen = self.obj_window.combo1.get(): It retrieves the currently selected item from the combo1 Combobox and stores it in the chosen variable.
2. self.obj_plot.choose_category(self.df_dummy, chosen, self.obj_window.figure1, self.obj_window.canvas1, self.obj_window.figure2, self.obj_window.canvas2): It calls the choose_category method of the self.obj_plot object (an instance of the Helper_Plot class) and passes several arguments to it:
    *   self.df_dummy: The DataFrame containing the categorized data.
    *   chosen: The selected item from combo1.
    *   self.obj_window.figure1 and self.obj_window.canvas1: Figure and canvas objects for plotting in the first section of the application.

- self.obj_window.figure2 and self.obj_window.canvas2: Figure and canvas objects for plotting in the second section of the application.

The purpose of this function is to respond to the user's selection from combo1 and trigger the appropriate plotting or visualization action based on the chosen item. The choose_category() method in the Helper_Plot class will determine which specific visualization to generate based on the chosen category. This approach makes the application interactive, allowing the user to explore different visualizations based on their selection.

Then, define a new method named choose_category() in Helper_Plot class:

```
def choose_category(self, df, chosen, figure1, canvas1, figure2, canvas2):
    if chosen == "Categorized Income versus Response":
        self.dist_one_vs_another_plot(df, "Income", "Response", figure1, canvas1, chosen)
```

This function takes several parameters, including a DataFrame (df), a string chosen, and four objects related to plotting (figure1, canvas1, figure2, canvas2). Its purpose is to enable the selection of different visualizations based on the user's choice from the chosen variable.

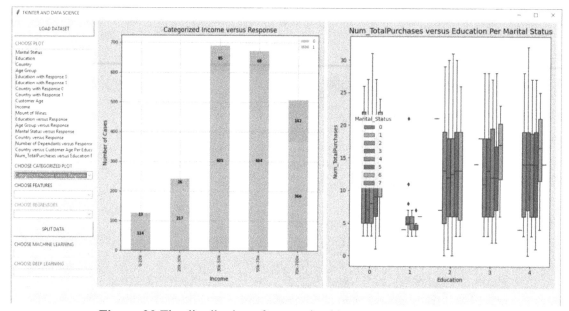

Figure 20 The distribution of categorized income versus response

In this specific code block, there is a single conditional branch that checks if the value of chosen is equal to "Categorized Income versus Response." If this condition is met, it invokes the dist_one_vs_another_plot() function to create a particular type of plot. The purpose of this visualization is to compare the categorized income levels of customers ("Income") with their response behavior ("Response"). This comparison can help analyze how different income categories are associated with customer responses, which is essential for understanding customer behavior and tailoring marketing strategies or product offerings accordingly. The result is shown in figure 20.

Distribution of Categorized Total Purchase versus Categorized Income

Add this code to the end of choose_category() method in Helper_Plot class:

```
if chosen == "Categorized Total Purchase versus Categorized Income":
    self.dist_one_vs_another_plot(df, "Num_TotalPurchases", "Income", figure2, canvas2, chosen)
```

The purpose of this code is to enable an interactive data exploration feature within an application. When the user selects this particular option, the code generates a specific type of plot that visually represents the relationship between categorized total purchases and categorized income. This can help users gain insights into how these two variables are related within the dataset, allowing for data-driven decision-making and exploration. The result is shown in figure 21.

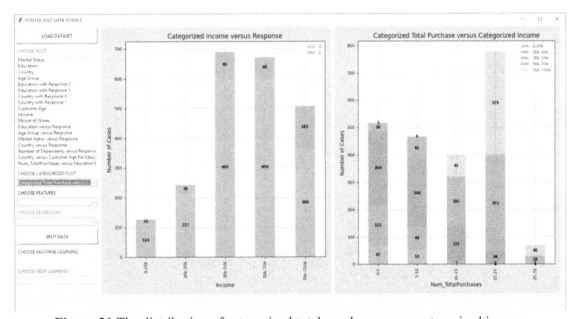

Figure 21 The distribution of categorized total purchase versus categorized income

Distribution of Categorized Recency versus Categorized Total Purchase

Add this code to the end of choose_category() method in Helper_Plot class:

```
if chosen == "Categorized Recency versus Categorized Total Purchase":
    self.dist_one_vs_another_plot(df, "Recency", "Num_TotalPurchases", figure1, canvas1, chosen)
```

The purpose of the code is to create a specific data visualization when the user selects "Categorized Recency versus Categorized Total Purchase" from a user interface element (a dropdown or combo box). This specific visualization involves comparing two categorical variables: "Categorized Recency" and "Categorized Total Purchase."

The resulting plot allows viewers to understand how the distribution of total purchases varies across different recency categories. For example, it helps answer questions like:
- Are customers who made purchases within the last 10 days more to fall into a specific total purchase category?
- How does recency impact the distribution of total purchases?

By presenting this information visually, the plot makes it easier to identify trends and patterns within the data and draw insights related to the interaction between these two categorical variables. The result is shown in figure 22.

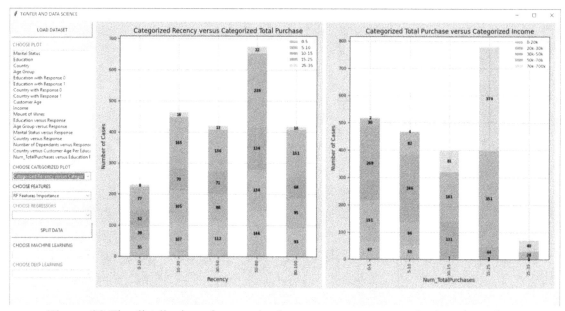

Figure 22 The distribution of categorized recency versus categorized total purchase

Distribution of Categorized Customer Month versus Categorized Customer Age

Add this code to the end of choose_category() method in Helper_Plot class:

```
if chosen == "Categorized Customer Month versus Categorized Customer Age":
    self.dist_one_vs_another_plot(df, "Dt_Customer_Month", "Customer_Age", figure2, canvas2, chosen)
```

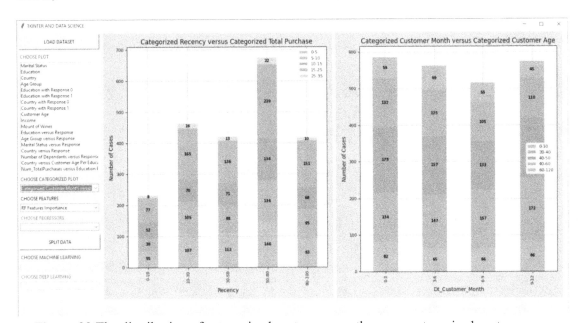

Figure 23 The distribution of categorized customer month versus categorized customer age

The purpose of the code is to create a visualization that shows the relationship between two categorical variables: "Categorized Customer Month" and "Categorized Customer Age." This visualization appears to be a stacked bar plot, and here's how it can be interpreted:

- X-Axis (Categorized Customer Month): The x-axis represents different categories or intervals for "Customer Month." These categories represent different months or groups of months in which customers joined or engaged with a service or product.
- Y-Axis (Count of Cases): The y-axis represents the count of cases or observations within each combination of "Categorized Customer Month" and "Categorized Customer Age." Each stacked bar on the plot represents the count of cases for a specific combination of these two categorical variables.
- Stacked Bars: Each category of "Categorized Customer Month" on the x-axis is depicted as a stacked bar. Within each stacked bar, there are segments or sections, each corresponding to a specific "Categorized Customer Age" category. The height of each

segment represents the count of cases that fall into that particular combination of month and age group.

This type of visualization helps in understanding how the distribution of customer ages varies across different months or periods when customers joined or engaged with a product or service. It allows viewers to explore whether certain months attract customers of specific age groups and whether there are any patterns or trends in the data related to these two categorical variables.

Distribution of Categorized Amount of Gold Products Purchased versus Categorized Income

Add this code to the end of choose_category() method in Helper_Plot class:

```
if chosen == "Categorized Amount of Gold Products versus Categorized Income":
    self.dist_one_vs_another_plot(df, "MntGoldProds", "Income", figure1, canvas1, chosen)
```

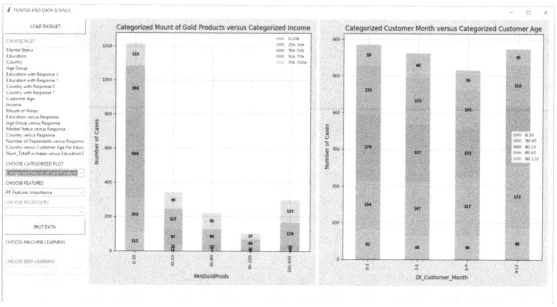

Figure 24 The distribution of categorized amount of gold Products purchased versus categorized income

The code segment serves the purpose of generating a stacked bar plot to visually depict the association between two distinct variables: "Categorized Amount of Gold Products" and "Categorized Income." This visualization is designed to offer insights into how customer income levels relate to their expenditure on gold products. The x-axis represents various categories or intervals delineating the amount spent on gold products, encompassing ranges like "0-30," "30-50," "50-80," and so forth. Meanwhile, the y-axis quantifies the number of cases or observations in each combination of "Categorized Amount of Gold Products" and "Categorized Income." Each stacked bar on the plot corresponds to a specific "Categorized Amount of Gold Products" category and portrays the count of cases for that precise amalgamation of these two categorical variables. These stacked bars further consist of segments, with each segment symbolizing a distinct "Categorized Income" category. The segment's height reflects the count of cases belonging to the particular combination of gold product spending and income category. Additionally, the plot is expected to feature a legend to elucidate the color coding associated with various "Categorized Income" categories, along with a title like "Categorized Amount of Gold Products versus Categorized Income" to succinctly convey the plot's focus. The result is shown figure 24.

This type of visual representation serves as a powerful exploratory tool, enabling an examination of potential trends or patterns within the data. It allows for the investigation of whether individuals with higher incomes exhibit greater expenditures on gold products compared to those with lower incomes. Moreover, it facilitates the identification of any disparities in spending behaviors on gold products across different income groups. Through this visualization, one can gain valuable insights into consumer preferences and behaviors, which can be instrumental for data-driven decision-making in marketing or business strategies.

Distribution of Categorized Amount of Fish Products Purchased versus Categorized Total Amount Spent

Add this code to the end of choose_category() method in Helper_Plot class:

```
if chosen == "Categorized Amount of Fish Products versus Categorized Total AmountSpent":
    self.dist_one_vs_another_plot(df, "MntFishProducts", "TotalAmount_Spent", figure2, canvas2, chosen)
```

The code is responsible for generating a visual representation in the form of a histogram comparing two distinct variables: "Categorized Amount of Fish Products" and "Categorized Total Amount Spent." This visualization aims to offer insights into the relationship between two aspects of customer behavior. The x-axis of the histogram delineates different categories or intervals representing the amount spent on fish products, such as "0-10," "10-20," "20-40," and so forth. Meanwhile, the y-axis quantifies the number of cases or observations falling within each combination of "Categorized Amount of Fish Products" and "Categorized Total Amount Spent." Each bar on the histogram corresponds to a specific category of "Categorized Amount of Fish Products" and represents the count of cases that belong to that particular combination of these two categorical variables. The height of each bar reflects the number of cases within that specific combination. This visualization aims to provide a clear and concise overview of how spending on fish products relates to the total amount spent by customers.

Histograms are valuable tools for visualizing the distribution and relationships between variables. In this specific context, this visualization enables a quick assessment of whether customers who spend more on fish products tend to have higher total expenditure or whether there are noticeable patterns in spending behavior. It also allows for the identification of any concentration of cases within specific combinations of spending categories. By creating this histogram, one can gain insights into customer preferences and spending habits, which can be valuable for marketing strategies and business decision-making.

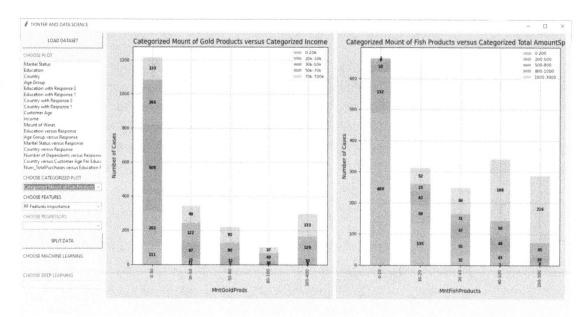

Figure 25 distribution of categorized amount of fish products purchased versus categorized total amount spent

Distribution of Categorized Amount of Meat Products Purchased versus Categorized Recency

Add this code to the end of choose_category() method in Helper_Plot class:

```
if chosen == "Categorized Amount of Meat Products versus Categorized Recency":
    self.dist_one_vs_another_plot(df, "MntMeatProducts", "Recency", figure1, canvas1, chosen)
```

The code is responsible for generating a visual representation in the form of a histogram comparing two distinct variables: "Categorized Amount of Meat Products" and "Categorized Recency." This visualization aims to offer insights into the relationship between these two aspects of customer behavior. The x-axis of the histogram consists of different categories or intervals representing the amount spent on meat products, such as "0-50," "50-100," "100-200," and so forth. Meanwhile, the y-axis quantifies the number of cases or observations falling within each combination of "Categorized Amount of Meat Products" and "Categorized Recency." Each bar on the histogram corresponds to a specific category of "Categorized Amount of Meat Products" and represents the count of cases that belong to that particular combination of these two categorical variables. The height of each bar reflects the number of cases within that specific combination. This visualization aims to provide a clear and concise overview of how spending on meat products relates to the recency of customer interactions.

Histograms are valuable tools for visualizing the distribution and relationships between variables. In this specific context, this visualization enables a quick assessment of whether customers who spend more on meat products tend to have more recent interactions or whether there are noticeable patterns in spending behavior concerning recency. It also allows for the identification of any concentration of cases within specific combinations of spending categories and recency intervals. By creating this histogram, one can gain insights into customer preferences and spending habits relative to the recency of their interactions, which can be valuable for marketing strategies and business decision-making.

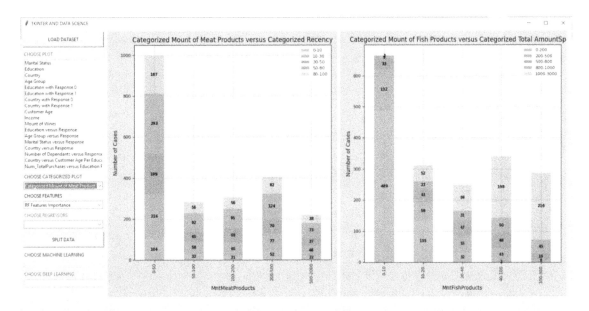

Figure 26 distribution of categorized amount of meat products purchased versus categorized recency

Plotting Correlation Matrix
Add a new method named plot_corr_mat() in Helper_Plot class:

```
def plot_corr_mat(self, df, figure, canvas):
    figure.clear()
    plot1 = figure.add_subplot(1,1,1)
    categorical_columns = df.select_dtypes(include=['object', 'category']).columns
    df_removed = df.drop(columns=categorical_columns)
    corrdata = df_removed.corr()

    annot_kws = {"size": 5}
    sns.heatmap(corrdata, ax = plot1, lw=1, annot=True, cmap="Reds", annot_kws=annot_kws)
    plot1.set_title('Correlation Matrix', fontweight ="bold",fontsize=14)

    # Set font for x and y labels
    plot1.set_xlabel('Features', fontweight="bold", fontsize=12)
    plot1.set_ylabel('Features', fontweight="bold", fontsize=12)

    # Set font for tick labels
    plot1.tick_params(axis='both', which='major', labelsize=5)
    plot1.tick_params(axis='both', which='minor', labelsize=5)

    figure.tight_layout()
    canvas.draw()
```

The code generates a correlation matrix heatmap to visualize the relationships between numerical features in a dataset. Here are the steps of the code:

1. Clear Existing Plot:
    The function begins by clearing any existing content on the specified figure to ensure a clean canvas for the new plot.
2. Create a Subplot:
    A subplot is added to the figure using figure.add_subplot(1, 1, 1). This creates a single subplot in a 1x1 grid for the correlation matrix heatmap.
3. Select Categorical Columns:
    The code identifies and selects the categorical columns in the DataFrame using df.select_dtypes(include=['object', 'category']).columns. These categorical columns are excluded from the correlation matrix calculation as they are not numerical.
4. Remove Categorical Columns:
    The selected categorical columns are removed from the DataFrame using df.drop(columns=categorical_columns). This creates a new DataFrame (df_removed) containing only numerical features.
5. Calculate Correlation Matrix:
    The code calculates the correlation matrix for the numerical features in df_removed using corrdata = df_removed.corr(). This matrix contains pairwise correlations between all numerical features.
6. Customize Heatmap:

- annot_kws is a dictionary specifying additional attributes for the annotations on the heatmap. In this case, it sets the annotation text size to 5.
- sns.heatmap() is used to create the heatmap, and it is plotted on the previously created subplot (ax=plot1).
- The annot=True argument ensures that the correlation values are displayed on the heatmap.
- The cmap argument specifies the color map for the heatmap, and in this case, "Reds" is used.
- The annot_kws dictionary is passed to customize annotation attributes.

7. Set Titles and Labels:
    - The title of the plot is set to 'Correlation Matrix' with specified font properties.
    - Labels for the x and y axes are set with font properties to indicate that the features represent the same set of features on both axes.

8. Adjust Tick Labels:
    The tick labels for both major and minor ticks on the plot's axes are adjusted to have a font size of 5.

9. Tight Layout:
    figure.tight_layout() is called to ensure that the plot layout is adjusted to fit properly within the figure.

10. Draw the Plot:
    Finally, canvas.draw() is called to render and display the correlation matrix heatmap on the canvas within the user interface.

Then, add this code to the end of binds_event() method in Main_Class:

```
# Binds combobox2 to a function
self.obj_window.combo2.bind("<<ComboboxSelected>>", self.choose_combobox2)
```

This line of code binds a function to an event for a specific Combobox (dropdown) widget in a graphical user interface (GUI) application, typically created using the tkinter library in Python.

Here's an explanation of this line of code:

- self.obj_window.combo2: This part of the code references a Combobox widget (combo2) that is part of the obj_window object, which appears to be an instance of a custom window design class. This Combobox widget is used to display a list of options that the user can choose from.
- .bind("<<ComboboxSelected>>", self.choose_combobox2): This part of the code uses the bind method to associate a function (self.choose_combobox2) with the event generated when an item is selected in the Combobox. The event being bound to is

"<<ComboboxSelected>>", which is a predefined event in tkinter that is triggered when the user selects an item from the Combobox dropdown list.

- self.choose_combobox2: This is the function that will be executed when the event (item selection in the Combobox) occurs. It appears that this function is responsible for handling the user's choice and performing specific actions based on the selected item.

In summary, this line of code sets up an event-handler mechanism for the second Combobox (combo2) in the GUI application. When the user selects an item from this Combobox, the self.choose_combobox2 function will be called to respond to the user's selection, possibly by updating the GUI or performing other relevant actions based on the selected item.

Next, add a new method named choose_combobox2() in Main_Class:

```
def choose_combobox2(self, event):
    chosen = self.obj_window.combo2.get()
    self.obj_plot.choose_plot_more(self.df_final, chosen,
        self.X, self.y,
        self.obj_window.figure1,
        self.obj_window.canvas1, self.obj_window.figure2,
        self.obj_window.canvas2)
```

This code defines a function named choose_combobox2() that serves as an event handler for a Combobox (combo2) in a graphical user interface (GUI) application, created using the tkinter library in Python. Here's an explanation of what this function does:

1. event: This function takes an event parameter, which represents the event that triggered the function's execution. In this case, the event is the selection of an item in combo2.
2. chosen = self.obj_window.combo2.get(): Within the function, it retrieves the currently selected item from combo2 using the get() method. This selected item is stored in the chosen variable.
3. self.obj_plot.choose_plot_more(...): This line of code calls a method named choose_plot_more on an instance of the obj_plot object. It passes several arguments to this method, including:
   - self.df_final: The dataset, which is expected to be a Pandas DataFrame.
   - chosen: The selected item from combo2.
   - self.X and self.y: Input and output variables used for data plotting or analysis.
   - self.obj_window.figure1, self.obj_window.canvas1, self.obj_window.figure2, self.obj_window.canvas2: These appear to be graphical components (e.g., Matplotlib figures and canvases) associated with the GUI.

The choose_plot_more() method in obj_plot is expected to handle the selected item and possibly generate plots, display data, or perform other relevant actions based on the user's choice. This function essentially bridges the user's interaction with the GUI Combobox (combo2) and the corresponding data visualization or analysis functionality provided by the obj_plot object.

Then, in Helper_Plot class, define a new method named choose_plot_more():

```
def choose_plot_more(self, df, chosen, X, y, figure1, canvas1, figure2, canvas2):
    if chosen == "Correlation Matrix":
        self.plot_corr_mat(df, figure1, canvas1)
```

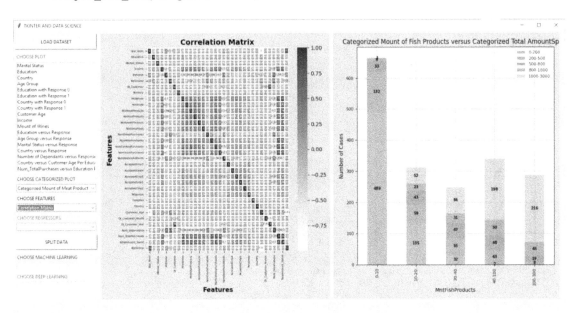

Figure 27 The correlation matrix

The choose_plot_more() method is a part of the application that allows users to select different types of plots or visualizations. This method handles the user's choice and calls the appropriate plotting function based on the chosen option. Here's an explanation of what this specific code block does:

1. chosen: This parameter represents the user's choice, which is the type of plot or visualization they want to see. It is passed as an argument to the method.

2. Inside the method, there is an if statement that checks the value of chosen. Depending on the value of chosen, a specific plotting function is called.

3. In this code block, if the chosen value is "Correlation Matrix," the method calls another function named plot_corr_mat() with the following arguments:

   • df: The dataset (presumably a Pandas DataFrame) on which the correlation matrix is calculated and visualized.

   • figure1: A Matplotlib figure where the correlation matrix plot will be displayed.

   • canvas1: A Matplotlib canvas associated with figure1 for rendering the plot.

The plot_corr_mat() function is expected to generate a heatmap-based correlation matrix plot for the given dataset and display it in the specified figure and canvas.

This code structure allows users to select different types of plots from a Combobox in the GUI, and the appropriate plotting function is executed based on their selection. In this case, it handles the "Correlation Matrix" option, as shown in figure 27.

Plotting Feature Importance Using Random Forest Classifier

Add a new method named plot_rf_importance() in Helper_Plot class:

```
def plot_rf_importance(self, X, y, figure, canvas):
    result_rf = self.obj_data.feat_importance_rf(X, y)
    figure.clear()
    plot1 = figure.add_subplot(1,1,1)
    sns.set_color_codes("pastel")
    ax=sns.barplot(x = 'Values',y = 'Features', data=result_rf, color="Blue", ax=plot1)
    plot1.set_title('Random Forest Features Importance', fontweight ="bold",fontsize=14)

    plot1.set_xlabel('Features Importance', fontsize=10)
    plot1.set_ylabel('Feature Labels', fontsize=10)
    # Set font for tick labels
    plot1.tick_params(axis='both', which='major', labelsize=5)
    plot1.tick_params(axis='both', which='minor', labelsize=5)
    figure.tight_layout()
    canvas.draw()
```

The plot_rf_importance() method is used to generate and display a bar plot showing the feature importance scores obtained from a Random Forest model. Below is a step-by-step explanation of what this code does:

1. X and y: These parameters represent the input features (independent variables) and target variable (dependent variable) for a machine learning model. The feature importance scores will be calculated based on these variables.

2. figure and canvas: These parameters represent a Matplotlib figure and canvas, respectively. The figure is where the bar plot will be displayed, and the canvas is associated with the figure for rendering the plot.

3. The method first calculates the feature importances using the feat_importance_rf method from the obj_data object. This method presumably fits a Random Forest classifier on the provided data (X and y) and returns the feature importances.

4. The figure is cleared using figure.clear(), ensuring that it's ready to display the new plot.

5. A subplot is added to the figure using figure.add_subplot(1, 1, 1). This creates a single subplot within the figure.

6. Matplotlib's sns.barplot function is used to create a bar plot. It takes the following arguments:
   - x='Values' and y='Features': These specify the data to be plotted on the x and y-axes. In this case, the feature importance scores are on the x-axis, and feature labels are on the y-axis.
   - data=result_rf: The data source for the plot, where result_rf is assumed to be a DataFrame containing feature names and their importance scores.
   - color="Blue": This sets the color of the bars in the bar plot.
7. Titles and labels are set for the plot:
   - plot1.set_title(...): Sets the title of the plot.
   - plot1.set_xlabel(...): Sets the x-axis label.
   - plot1.set_ylabel(...): Sets the y-axis label.
8. Tick parameters are adjusted to set the font size for tick labels using plot1.tick_params(...). This helps improve the readability of the plot.
9. The figure is tightly formatted using figure.tight_layout() to ensure that all elements of the plot fit nicely within the figure.
10. Finally, canvas.draw() is called to render the plot on the associated canvas.

Overall, this method allows you to visualize and explore the feature importance scores obtained from a Random Forest model using a bar plot.

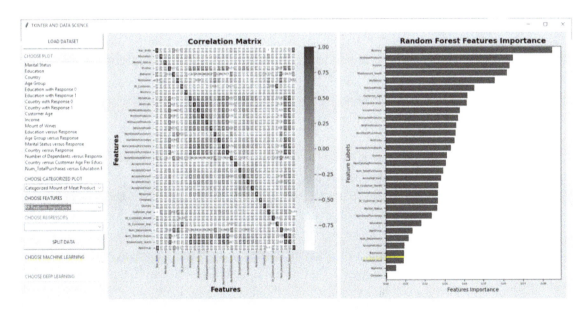

Figure 28 The Random Forest feature importance

Add this code to the end of choose_plot_more() in Helper_Plot class:

```
if chosen == "RF Features Importance":
    self.plot_rf_importance(X, y, figure2, canvas2)
```

Then, run main_class.py. Choose, "RF Features Importance" in second combobox to see Random Forest feature importance as shown in figure 28.

Plotting Feature Importance Using Extra Trees Classifier

Add a new method named plot_et_importance() in Helper_Plot class:

```
def plot_et_importance(self, X, y, figure, canvas):
    result_rf = self.obj_data.feat_importance_et(X, y)
    figure.clear()
    plot1 = figure.add_subplot(1,1,1)
    sns.set_color_codes("pastel")
    ax=sns.barplot(x = 'Values',y = 'Features', data=result_rf, color="Red", ax=plot1)
    plot1.set_title('Extra Trees Features Importance', fontweight ="bold",fontsize=14)

    plot1.set_xlabel('Features Importance',  fontsize=10)
    plot1.set_ylabel('Feature Labels',  fontsize=10)
    # Set font for tick labels
    plot1.tick_params(axis='both', which='major', labelsize=5)
    plot1.tick_params(axis='both', which='minor', labelsize=5)
    figure.tight_layout()
    canvas.draw()
```

The plot_et_importance() method is similar to the previously explained plot_rf_importance() method but is used to generate and display a bar plot showing the feature importance scores obtained from an Extra Trees model (another ensemble machine learning algorithm). Here's a step-by-step explanation of what this code does:

1. X and y: These parameters represent the input features (independent variables) and target variable (dependent variable) for a machine learning model. The feature importance scores will be calculated based on these variables.
2. figure and canvas: These parameters represent a Matplotlib figure and canvas, respectively. The figure is where the bar plot will be displayed, and the canvas is associated with the figure for rendering the plot.
3. The method first calculates the feature importances using the feat_importance_et() method from the obj_data object. This method presumably fits an Extra Trees classifier on the provided data (X and y) and returns the feature importances.
4. The figure is cleared using figure.clear(), ensuring that it's ready to display the new plot.
5. A subplot is added to the figure using figure.add_subplot(1, 1, 1). This creates a single subplot within the figure.

6. Matplotlib's sns.barplot function is used to create a bar plot, similar to the previous explanation. It specifies the data for the x-axis, y-axis, data source, and bar color.

7. Titles and labels are set for the plot, similar to the previous explanation.

8. Tick parameters are adjusted to set the font size for tick labels using plot1.tick_params(...), just like in the previous method.

9. The figure is tightly formatted using figure.tight_layout() to ensure that all elements of the plot fit nicely within the figure.

10. Finally, canvas.draw() is called to render the plot on the associated canvas.

In summary, this method allows you to visualize and explore the feature importance scores obtained from an Extra Trees model using a bar plot, providing insights into which features are most influential for the model's predictions.

Add this code to the end of choose_plot_more() in Helper_Plot class:

```
if chosen == "ET Features Importance":
    self.plot_et_importance(X, y, figure2, canvas2)
```

Then, run main_class.py. Choose, "ET Features Importance" in second combobox to see Random Forest feature importance as shown in figure 29.

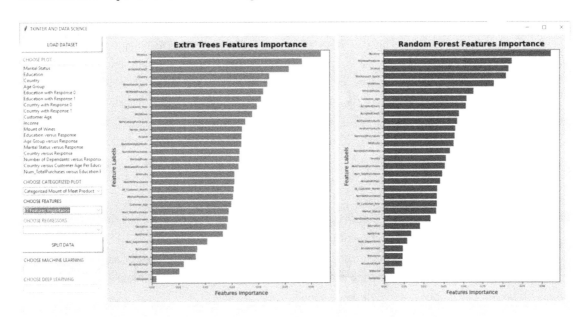

Figure 29 The Extra Trees feature importance

Plotting Feature Importance Using Recursive Feature Elimination (RFE)

Add a new method named plot_rfe_importance() in Helper_Plot class:

```python
def plot_rfe_importance(self, X, y, figure, canvas):
    result_lg = self.obj_data.feat_importance_rfe(X, y)
    figure.clear()
    plot1 = figure.add_subplot(1,1,1)
    sns.set_color_codes("pastel")
    ax=sns.barplot(x = 'Ranking',y = 'Features', data=result_lg, color="orange", ax=plot1)
    plot1.set_title('RFE Features Importance', fontweight ="bold",fontsize=14)

    plot1.set_xlabel('Features Importance',  fontsize=10)
    plot1.set_ylabel('Feature Labels',  fontsize=10)
    # Set font for tick labels
    plot1.tick_params(axis='both', which='major', labelsize=5)
    plot1.tick_params(axis='both', which='minor', labelsize=5)
    figure.tight_layout()
    canvas.draw()
```

The plot_rfe_importance() method is used to generate and display a bar plot showing the feature ranking obtained from a Recursive Feature Elimination (RFE) process using a Logistic Regression model. Here's a step-by-step explanation of what this code does:

1. X and y: These parameters represent the input features (independent variables) and target variable (dependent variable) for a machine learning model. The feature rankings will be calculated based on these variables.

2. figure and canvas: These parameters represent a Matplotlib figure and canvas, respectively. The figure is where the bar plot will be displayed, and the canvas is associated with the figure for rendering the plot.

3. The method first calculates the feature rankings using the feat_importance_rfe method from the obj_data object. This method presumably performs RFE with a Logistic Regression model on the provided data (X and y) and returns the feature rankings.

4. The figure is cleared using figure.clear(), ensuring that it's ready to display the new plot.

5. A subplot is added to the figure using figure.add_subplot(1, 1, 1). This creates a single subplot within the figure.

6. Matplotlib's sns.barplot function is used to create a bar plot. It specifies the data for the x-axis, y-axis, data source, and bar color.

7. Titles and labels are set for the plot, similar to the previous explanations.

8. Tick parameters are adjusted to set the font size for tick labels using plot1.tick_params(...), just like in the previous methods.

9. The figure is tightly formatted using figure.tight_layout() to ensure that all elements of the plot fit nicely within the figure.

10. Finally, canvas.draw() is called to render the plot on the associated canvas.

In summary, this method allows you to visualize and explore the feature rankings obtained from an RFE process using a Logistic Regression model. The bar plot provides insights into the importance of each feature based on their ranking. Features with lower rankings are considered more important for the model.

Add this code to the end of choose_plot_more() in Helper_Plot class:

```
if chosen == "RFE Features Importance":
    self.plot_rfe_importance(X, y, figure2, canvas2)
```

Then, run main_class.py. Choose, "ET Features Importance" in second combobox to see Random Forest feature importance as shown in figure 30.

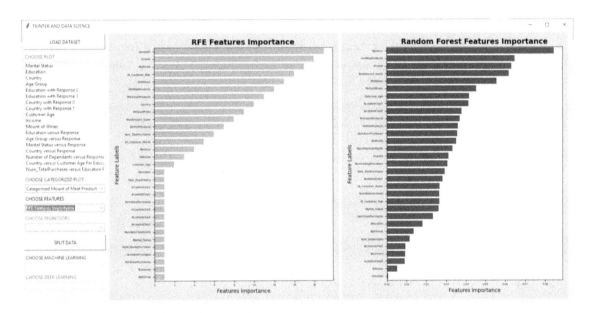

Figure 30 The RFE feature importance

MACHINE LEARNING MODELS

Machine_Learning Class

Create a new python file name machine_learning.py. In it, create a class named Machine_Learning. It is part of a machine learning workflow and is responsible for training and evaluating various classification models. Let's break down its main components and responsibilities:

- Imports: The class imports various libraries and modules necessary for machine learning tasks. These include libraries for data preprocessing, model selection, evaluation metrics, and specific machine learning algorithms.
- Initialization: The class's constructor initializes an instance of the Process_Data class as self.obj_data. The Process_Data class contains methods for data preprocessing and feature engineering.

```python
#machine_learning.py
import numpy as np
from imblearn.over_sampling import SMOTE
from sklearn.model_selection import train_test_split, RandomizedSearchCV, GridSearchCV,
StratifiedKFold
from sklearn.preprocessing import StandardScaler
import joblib
from sklearn.linear_model import LogisticRegression
from sklearn.metrics import confusion_matrix, accuracy_score, recall_score, precision_score
from sklearn.metrics import classification_report, f1_score, plot_confusion_matrix
from sklearn.ensemble import RandomForestClassifier
from sklearn.neighbors import KNeighborsClassifier
from sklearn.tree import DecisionTreeClassifier
from sklearn.ensemble import AdaBoostClassifier, GradientBoostingClassifier
from xgboost import XGBClassifier
from sklearn.neural_network import MLPClassifier
from sklearn.svm import SVC
import os
import joblib
import pandas as pd
from process_data import Process_Data

class Machine_Learning:
    def __init__(self):
```

```
self.obj_data = Process_Data()
```

Oversampling and Splitting Data

In Machine_Learning class, define a new method named oversampling_splitting() as follows:

```python
def oversampling_splitting(self, X, y):
    sm = SMOTE(random_state=42)
    X,y = sm.fit_resample(X, y.ravel())

    #Splits the data into training and testing
    X_train, X_test, y_train, y_test = train_test_split(X, y, test_size = 0.2, random_state = 2021,
stratify=y)

    #Use Standard Scaler
    scaler = StandardScaler()
    X_train_stand = scaler.fit_transform(X_train)
    X_test_stand = scaler.transform(X_test)

    #Saves into pkl files
    joblib.dump(X_train_stand, 'X_train.pkl')
    joblib.dump(X_test_stand, 'X_test.pkl')
    joblib.dump(y_train, 'y_train.pkl')
    joblib.dump(y_test, 'y_test.pkl')
```

The oversampling_splitting() method within the Machine_Learning class performs the following tasks:

1. Oversampling: It uses the Synthetic Minority Over-sampling Technique (SMOTE) to address class imbalance. SMOTE generates synthetic samples of the minority class to balance the class distribution. This is done to prevent the model from being biased towards the majority class. The resulting oversampled dataset is stored in X and y.

2. Train-Test Split: After oversampling, the method splits the dataset into training and testing sets using train_test_split from sklearn.model_selection. The test_size parameter controls the proportion of data allocated to the test set (in this case, 20% of the data), and stratify=y ensures that the class distribution is preserved in both the training and testing sets.

3. Feature Scaling: It scales the features in both the training and testing sets using StandardScaler from sklearn.preprocessing. Feature scaling is essential to ensure that all features have the same scale, which can improve the performance of many machine learning algorithms.

4. Saving Data: Finally, the method saves the scaled training and testing data, as well as the corresponding labels (y_train and y_test), into separate pickle (pkl) files. These files can be used for training and evaluating machine learning models in the future without the need to perform data preprocessing again.

Overall, the oversampling_splitting() method prepares the data for machine learning by addressing class imbalance, splitting it into training and testing sets, performing feature scaling, and saving the preprocessed data for later use. This is a critical step in the machine learning workflow to ensure that models are trained on appropriate data and can be easily reused for predictions.

Loading Files

In Machine_Learning class, define a new method named loading_files() as follows:

```python
def load_files(self):
    X_train = joblib.load('X_train.pkl')
    X_test = joblib.load('X_test.pkl')
    y_train = joblib.load('y_train.pkl')
    y_test = joblib.load('y_test.pkl')

    return X_train, X_test, y_train, y_test
```

The load_files() method in the Machine_Learning class is responsible for loading the preprocessed training and testing data from pickle (pkl) files that were previously saved using the oversampling_splitting method. Here's what this method does:

1. Loading Data: It uses the joblib.load function to load the following data files:
    - X_train.pkl: This file contains the preprocessed and scaled features (X) of the training dataset.
    - X_test.pkl: This file contains the preprocessed and scaled features (X) of the testing dataset.
    - y_train.pkl: This file contains the labels (y) corresponding to the training dataset.
    - y_test.pkl: This file contains the labels (y) corresponding to the testing dataset.
2. Return Data: After loading these files, the method returns four variables:
    - X_train: The preprocessed and scaled features of the training dataset.
    - X_test: The preprocessed and scaled features of the testing dataset.
    - y_train: The labels corresponding to the training dataset.
    - y_test: The labels corresponding to the testing dataset.

The purpose of this method is to provide a convenient way to access the preprocessed data, which can then be used for training and evaluating machine learning models without the need to perform data preprocessing again. This separation of data loading and preprocessing from the modeling process makes it easier to maintain and reuse machine learning pipelines.

Training Model and Predicting Result

In Machine_Learning class, define two new methods named train_model() and predict_model() as follows:

```
def train_model(self, model, X, y):
    model.fit(X, y)
    return model

def predict_model(self, model, X, proba=False):
    if ~proba:
        y_pred = model.predict(X)
    else:
        y_pred_proba = model.predict_proba(X)
        y_pred = np.argmax(y_pred_proba, axis=1)

    return y_pred
```

The train_model() and predict_model() methods in the Machine_Learning class are responsible for training a machine learning model and making predictions using that trained model. Here's an explanation of each method:

1. train_model(self, model, X, y)

   This method takes three arguments:

   - model: The machine learning model to be trained.
   - X: The feature matrix (input data) for training.
   - y: The target labels for training.

2. Inside the method, the fit function is called on the provided model with the input feature matrix X and target labels y. This step trains the machine learning model on the provided training data.

3. Finally, the trained model is returned as the output of the method.

4. predict_model(self, model, X, proba=False)

   This method takes three arguments:

   - model: The trained machine learning model for making predictions.
   - X: The feature matrix (input data) for which predictions are to be made.
   - proba (optional, default is False): A boolean flag indicating whether to return class probabilities (True) or class labels (False) as predictions.

5. If proba is False, the method uses the predict function of the model to make class label predictions based on the input features X. The predicted class labels are stored in the y_pred variable.

6. If proba is True, the method uses the predict_proba function of the model to obtain class probabilities for each class. It then selects the class with the highest probability as the predicted class label and stores it in the y_pred variable.

7. The predicted class labels (or probabilities) are returned as the output of the method.

These methods are generic and can be used with various machine learning models for tasks such as classification. They provide a consistent way to train models and make predictions, making it easier to switch between different models and evaluate their performance.

Running Model

In Machine_Learning class, define a new method named run_model() as follows:

```python
def run_model(self, name, model, X_train, X_test, y_train, y_test, proba=False):
    y_pred = self.predict_model(model, X_test, proba)

    accuracy = accuracy_score(y_test, y_pred)
    recall = recall_score(y_test, y_pred, average='weighted')
    precision = precision_score(y_test, y_pred, average='weighted')
    f1 = f1_score(y_test, y_pred, average='weighted')

    print(name)
    print('accuracy: ', accuracy)
    print('recall: ', recall)
    print('precision: ', precision)
    print('f1: ', f1)
    print(classification_report(y_test, y_pred))

    return y_pred
```

The run_model() method in the Machine_Learning class is responsible for running a trained machine learning model on a test dataset and evaluating its performance. Here's an explanation of the method:

1. run_model(self, name, model, X_train, X_test, y_train, y_test, proba=False)
   This method takes several arguments:
   - name: A string representing the name or identifier for the model being evaluated.
   - model: The trained machine learning model to be evaluated.
   - X_train: The feature matrix of the training data.
   - X_test: The feature matrix of the testing data.
   - y_train: The target labels of the training data.
   - y_test: The target labels of the testing data.
   - proba (optional, default is False): A boolean flag indicating whether to return class probabilities (True) or class labels (False) as predictions.
2. Inside the method, the predict_model() method is called to obtain predictions from the model on the test data X_test.
3. Several evaluation metrics are calculated based on the predicted labels and the true labels (y_test). These metrics include:
   - Accuracy: The proportion of correctly predicted labels.
   - Recall: A weighted average of the recall scores for each class.
   - Precision: A weighted average of the precision scores for each class.

- F1-score: A weighted average of the F1-scores for each class.

4. The method then prints the model's name, along with the calculated metrics, to provide an overview of its performance.

5. Finally, the method returns the predicted labels (y_pred). This can be useful for further analysis or visualization.

The run_model() method serves as a standardized way to evaluate and compare different machine learning models on the same dataset, making it easier to assess their effectiveness for a given task.

Plotting Confusion Matrix and ROC

In Helper_Plot class, define a new method named plot_cm_roc() as follows:

```
def plot_cm_roc(self, model, X_test, y_test, ypred, name, figure, canvas):
    figure.clear()

    #Plots confusion matrix
    plot1 = figure.add_subplot(2,1,1)
    cm = confusion_matrix(y_test, ypred, )
    sns.heatmap(cm, annot=True, linewidth=3, linecolor='red', fmt='g', cmap="Greens",
annot_kws={"size": 14}, ax=plot1)
    plot1.set_title('Confusion Matrix' + " of " + name, fontsize=12)
    plot1.set_xlabel('Y predict', fontsize=10)
    plot1.set_ylabel('Y test', fontsize=10)
    plot1.xaxis.set_ticklabels(['Responsive', 'Not Responsive'], fontsize=10)
    plot1.yaxis.set_ticklabels(['Responsive', 'Not Responsive'], fontsize=10)

    #Plots ROC
    plot2 = figure.add_subplot(2,1,2)
    Y_pred_prob = model.predict_proba(X_test)
    Y_pred_prob = Y_pred_prob[:, 1]

    fpr, tpr, thresholds = roc_curve(y_test, Y_pred_prob)
    plot2.plot([0,1],[0,1], color='navy', linestyle='--', linewidth=3)
    plot2.plot(fpr,tpr, color='red', linewidth=3)
    plot2.set_xlabel('False Positive Rate', fontsize=10)
    plot2.set_ylabel('True Positive Rate', fontsize=10)
    plot2.set_title('ROC Curve of ' + name , fontsize=12)
    plot2.grid(True)

    figure.tight_layout()
    canvas.draw()
```

The plot_cm_roc() method in the Helper_Plot class is responsible for plotting two key visualizations for model evaluation: the confusion matrix and the Receiver Operating Characteristic (ROC) curve. Here's an explanation of the method:

1. plot_cm_roc(self, model, X_test, y_test, ypred, name, figure, canvas)
   This method takes several arguments:
   - model: The trained machine learning model to be evaluated.
   - X_test: The feature matrix of the testing data.
   - y_test: The target labels of the testing data.
   - ypred: The predicted labels obtained from the model on the test data.
   - name: A string representing the name or identifier for the model being evaluated.
   - figure: A Matplotlib figure object where the visualizations will be plotted.
   - canvas: A Matplotlib canvas object associated with the figure.
2. Inside the method, two subplots are created within the specified figure. These subplots are used to display the confusion matrix and the ROC curve side by side.
3. For the confusion matrix, seaborn is used to create a heatmap of the confusion matrix (cm). The heatmap includes annotations of the values within each cell, and the color map is set to "Greens." Axis labels and tick labels are added to the plot for clarity. The confusion matrix provides insights into the model's classification performance.
4. For the ROC curve, the method calculates the False Positive Rate (FPR) and True Positive Rate (TPR) using the roc_curve function. It then plots the ROC curve on the second subplot. The diagonal dashed line represents random guessing, and the red line represents the ROC curve of the model. The area under the ROC curve (AUC) is a common metric for assessing the model's discriminatory power.
5. The resulting plots for the confusion matrix and ROC curve are displayed in the specified figure. The canvas.draw() function is called to render and update the plots within the associated canvas.

This method provides a comprehensive visual summary of a model's performance, making it easier to assess both its classification accuracy (through the confusion matrix) and its ability to discriminate between classes (through the ROC curve).

Plotting True Values versus Predicted Values Diagram and Learning Curve

In Helper_Plot class, define a new method named plot_real_pred_val_learning_curve() as follows:

```python
#Plots true values versus predicted values diagram and learning curve
def plot_real_pred_val_learning_curve(self, model, X_train, y_train, X_test, y_test, ypred, name,
figure, canvas):
    figure.clear()

    #Plots true values versus predicted values diagram
    plot1 = figure.add_subplot(2,1,1)
    acc=accuracy_score(y_test, ypred)
    plot1.scatter(range(len(ypred)),ypred,color="blue", lw=3,label="Predicted")
    plot1.scatter(range(len(y_test)),
```

```
    y_test,color="red",label="Actual")
plot1.set_title("Predicted Values vs True Values of " + name, fontsize=12)
plot1.set_xlabel("Accuracy: " + str(round((acc*100),3)) + "%")
plot1.legend()
plot1.grid(True, alpha=0.75, lw=1, ls='-.')

#Plots learning curve
train_sizes=np.linspace(.1, 1.0, 5)
train_sizes, train_scores, test_scores, fit_times, _ = learning_curve(model,
    X_train, y_train, cv=None, n_jobs=None, train_sizes=train_sizes, return_times=True)
train_scores_mean = np.mean(train_scores, axis=1)
train_scores_std = np.std(train_scores, axis=1)
test_scores_mean = np.mean(test_scores, axis=1)
test_scores_std = np.std(test_scores, axis=1)

plot2 = figure.add_subplot(2,1,2)
plot2.fill_between(train_sizes, train_scores_mean - train_scores_std,
    train_scores_mean + train_scores_std, alpha=0.1, color="r")
plot2.fill_between(train_sizes, test_scores_mean - test_scores_std,
    test_scores_mean + test_scores_std, alpha=0.1, color="g")
plot2.plot(train_sizes, train_scores_mean, 'o-',
    color="r", label="Training score")
plot2.plot(train_sizes, test_scores_mean, 'o-',
    color="g", label="Cross-validation score")
plot2.legend(loc="best")
plot2.set_title("Learning curve of " + name, fontsize=12)
plot2.set_xlabel("fit_times")
plot2.set_ylabel("Score")
plot2.grid(True, alpha=0.75, lw=1, ls='-.')

figure.tight_layout()
canvas.draw()
```

The plot_real_pred_val_learning_curve() method in the Helper_Plot class is responsible for plotting two visualizations: a diagram comparing true values versus predicted values and a learning curve. Here's an explanation of the method:

1. plot_real_pred_val_learning_curve(self, model, X_train, y_train, X_test, y_test, ypred, name, figure, canvas)

   This method takes several arguments:
   - model: The trained machine learning model to be evaluated.
   - X_train: The feature matrix of the training data.
   - y_train: The target labels of the training data.
   - X_test: The feature matrix of the testing data.
   - y_test: The target labels of the testing data.
   - ypred: The predicted labels obtained from the model on the test data.
   - name: A string representing the name or identifier for the model being evaluated.

- figure: A Matplotlib figure object where the visualizations will be plotted.
- canvas: A Matplotlib canvas object associated with the figure.

2. Inside the method, two subplots are created within the specified figure. These subplots are used to display the diagram comparing true values versus predicted values and the learning curve side by side.

3. For the true values versus predicted values diagram, the method calculates the accuracy of the model's predictions and adds this information to the plot title. It then creates scatter plots for both the predicted values (in blue) and the actual values (in red). The legend indicates which points represent predicted and actual values. This diagram helps visualize how well the model's predictions align with the actual values.

4. For the learning curve, the method uses the learning_curve() function to calculate the training and cross-validation scores at different training set sizes. It then plots the learning curve, including shaded areas representing the standard deviation of scores. The learning curve helps assess the model's performance in terms of bias and variance as the training set size increases.

5. The resulting plots for the true values versus predicted values diagram and the learning curve are displayed in the specified figure. The canvas.draw() function is called to render and update the plots within the associated canvas.

These visualizations provide insights into both the model's predictive performance (through the true values versus predicted values diagram) and its ability to generalize (through the learning curve).

Logistic Regression Classifier and Grid Search

In Machine_Learning class, define a new method named logistic_regression() as follows:

```
def logistic_regression(self, name, X_train, X_test, y_train, y_test):
    #Logistic Regression Classifier
    # Define the parameter grid for the grid search
    param_grid = {
        'C': [0.01, 0.1, 1, 10],
        'penalty': ['none', 'l2'],
        'solver': ['newton-cg', 'lbfgs', 'liblinear', 'saga'],
    }

    # Initialize the Logistic Regression model
    logreg = LogisticRegression(max_iter=5000, random_state=2021)

    # Create GridSearchCV with the Logistic Regression model and the parameter grid
    grid_search = GridSearchCV(logreg, param_grid, cv=3, scoring='accuracy', n_jobs=-1)

    # Train and perform grid search
```

```
grid_search.fit(X_train, y_train)

# Get the best Logistic Regression model from the grid search
best_model = grid_search.best_estimator_

#Saves model
joblib.dump(best_model, 'LR_Model.pkl')

# Print the best hyperparameters found
print(f"Best Hyperparameters for LR:")
print(grid_search.best_params_)

return best_model
```

The logistic_regression() method in the Machine_Learning class is responsible for training a Logistic Regression classifier using hyperparameter tuning through grid search. Here's a step-by-step explanation of the method:

1. Method Arguments:
   - name: A string representing the name or identifier for the model being trained (e.g., "Logistic Regression").
   - X_train: The feature matrix of the training data.
   - X_test: The feature matrix of the testing data.
   - y_train: The target labels of the training data.
   - y_test: The target labels of the testing data.

2. Grid Search for Hyperparameter Tuning:
   A parameter grid (param_grid) is defined, specifying a range of hyperparameters for the Logistic Regression classifier. This includes different values for the regularization strength (C), penalty type (penalty), and solver method (solver).

3. Logistic Regression Model Initialization:
   A Logistic Regression classifier (logreg) is initialized with some configuration, including a maximum number of iterations and a random seed. The max_iter parameter is set to 5000 to ensure that the solver converges, and random_state is set to 2021 for reproducibility.

4. Grid Search with Cross-Validation:
   GridSearchCV is used to perform grid search with cross-validation. It takes the initialized Logistic Regression model (logreg), the parameter grid (param_grid), the number of cross-validation folds (cv=3), the scoring metric (scoring='accuracy'), and the option to parallelize the search (n_jobs=-1).

5. Training and Model Selection:
   The fit() method of the grid search object (grid_search) is called with the training data (X_train, y_train) to train multiple Logistic Regression models with different hyperparameter combinations.

6. Best Model Selection:

The best-performing Logistic Regression model with the optimal hyperparameters is obtained using grid_search.best_estimator_.

7. Model Saving:

The best-performing Logistic Regression model is saved to a pickle file named 'LR_Model.pkl' using the joblib.dump method. This allows the model to be reused later without retraining.

8. Printing Best Hyperparameters:

The method prints the best hyperparameters found during the grid search for the Logistic Regression classifier.

9. Return Value:

The best-performing Logistic Regression model is returned as the output of the method.

Overall, this method automates the process of hyperparameter tuning for a Logistic Regression classifier, ensuring that the model is trained with the best hyperparameters found during the grid search.

Then, in Machine_Learning class, define a new method named implement_LR() as follows:

```
def implement_LR(self, chosen, X_train, X_test, y_train, y_test):
    file_path = os.getcwd()+"/LR_Model.pkl"
    if os.path.exists(file_path):
        model = joblib.load('LR_Model.pkl')
        y_pred = self.run_model(chosen, model, X_train, X_test, y_train, y_test, proba=True)
    else:
        model = self.logistic_regression(chosen, X_train, X_test, y_train, y_test)
        y_pred = self.run_model(chosen, model, X_train, X_test, y_train, y_test, proba=True)

    #Saves result into excel file
    self.obj_data.save_result(y_test, y_pred, "results_LR.csv")

    print("Training Logistic Regression done...")
    return model, y_pred
```

The implement_LR() method in the Machine_Learning class is responsible for implementing the Logistic Regression classifier for a given dataset and chosen category (target variable). Here's a step-by-step explanation of the method:

1. Method Arguments:

   - chosen: A string representing the chosen category or target variable.
   - X_train: The feature matrix of the training data.
   - X_test: The feature matrix of the testing data.
   - y_train: The target labels of the training data.
   - y_test: The target labels of the testing data.

2. Checking for Pre-trained Model:
   The method checks if a pre-trained Logistic Regression model exists in the current working directory. This is done by constructing the file path to 'LR_Model.pkl' and using os.path.exists(file_path).

3. Model Loading or Training:
   - If a pre-trained model exists, it is loaded using joblib.load('LR_Model.pkl'). Otherwise, the logistic_regression method is called to train a new Logistic Regression model with hyperparameter tuning.
   - Whether the model is loaded or trained, it is stored in the model variable.

4. Model Evaluation and Prediction:
   - The run_model() method is called to evaluate the model's performance on the testing data (X_test, y_test). The proba parameter is set to True, indicating that probability scores for class predictions should be computed.
   - The predicted class probabilities or labels are stored in the y_pred variable.

5. Saving Model Results:
   The method uses the save_result() method from the Process_Data class (self.obj_data) to save the model's results, including actual and predicted labels, into an Excel file named 'results_LR.csv'.

6. Printing Status:
   A message is printed to indicate that the training or loading of the Logistic Regression model is complete.

7. Return Value:
   The trained or loaded Logistic Regression model (model) and the predicted class probabilities or labels (y_pred) are returned as output.

Overall, this method allows you to either load a pre-trained Logistic Regression model or train a new one based on the chosen category, and then evaluates its performance on the testing data while saving the results for further analysis.

Then, in Helper_Plot class, define a new method named choose_plot_ML() method as follows:

```
def choose_plot_ML(self, root, chosen, X_train, X_test, y_train, y_test, figure1, canvas1, figure2, canvas2):
    if chosen == "Logistic Regression":
        best_model, y_pred = self.obj_ml.implement_LR(chosen, X_train, X_test, y_train, y_test)

        #Plots confusion matrix and ROC
        self.plot_cm_roc(best_model, X_test, y_test, y_pred, chosen, figure1, canvas1)

        #Plots true values versus predicted values diagram and learning curve
```

```
self.plot_real_pred_val_learning_curve(best_model, X_train, y_train,
    X_test, y_test, y_pred, chosen, figure2, canvas2)

#Shows table of result
df_lr = self.obj_data.read_dataset("results_LR.csv")
self.shows_table(root, df_lr, 450, 750, "Y_test and Y_pred of Logistic Regression")
```

The choose_plot_ML() method is responsible for selecting and displaying specific plots and visualizations related to a chosen machine learning algorithm. Below is a breakdown of how this method works:

1. Method Arguments:
   - root: The root Tkinter window where the plots and tables will be displayed.
   - chosen: A string representing the chosen machine learning algorithm.
   - X_train: The feature matrix of the training data.
   - X_test: The feature matrix of the testing data.
   - y_train: The target labels of the training data.
   - y_test: The target labels of the testing data.
   - figure1: A Matplotlib figure object for the first set of plots.
   - canvas1: A Matplotlib canvas object associated with figure1.
   - figure2: A Matplotlib figure object for the second set of plots.
   - canvas2: A Matplotlib canvas object associated with figure2.

2. Conditional Block Based on the Chosen Algorithm:
   The method checks the value of the chosen variable to determine which machine learning algorithm has been selected.

3. Logistic Regression (Chosen Algorithm):
   - If the chosen algorithm is "Logistic Regression," the implement_LR method from the Machine_Learning class is called to either load a pre-trained model or train a new one, based on whether a model file exists.
   - The following visualizations and actions are performed for Logistic Regression:
     - Confusion matrix and ROC curve are plotted using plot_cm_roc().
     - A diagram showing true values versus predicted values and a learning curve is plotted using plot_real_pred_val_learning_curve().
     - The results, including actual and predicted labels, are read from a CSV file and displayed in a table using shows_table().

4. Displaying the Visualizations:
   The visualizations and tables generated for the selected machine learning algorithm are displayed within the Tkinter root window (root) for the user to interact with.

Overall, this method provides a modular and organized way to select a machine learning algorithm, train or load the model, and display relevant visualizations and result tables based on the chosen algorithm. It promotes clarity and ease of use when analyzing machine learning model performance.

Then, in Main_Class, define a new method named train_ML() as follows:

```
def train_ML(self):
    file_path = os.getcwd()+"/X_train.pkl"
    if os.path.exists(file_path):
        self.X_train, self.X_test, self.y_train, self.y_test = self.obj_ML.load_files()
    else:
        self.obj_ML.oversampling_splitting(self.X, self.y)
        self.X_train, self.X_test, self.y_train, self.y_test = self.obj_ML.load_files()

    print("Loading files done...")

    #turns on combo4 and combo5 after splitting is done
    self.obj_window.combo4['state'] = 'normal'
    self.obj_window.combo5['state'] = 'normal'

    self.obj_window.button2.config(state="disabled")
```

The train_ML() method serves the purpose of preparing the data for machine learning, which includes loading or generating the training and testing datasets. Below is a detailed explanation of this method's functionality:
1. Checking for Existing Data Files:
    The method first checks if the data files (X_train.pkl, X_test.pkl, y_train.pkl, and y_test.pkl) already exist in the current working directory. These files typically store preprocessed and split data to avoid the need for repeated data preprocessing.
2. File Existence Check:
    *   If the data files exist (os.path.exists(file_path) is True), the method loads the training and testing datasets using the load_files() method from the Machine_Learning class.
    *   If the data files do not exist, the method proceeds to the data preparation steps below.
3. Data Oversampling and Splitting (If Files Do Not Exist):
    *   If the data files do not exist, the method calls the oversampling_splitting() method from the Machine_Learning class. This method performs the following steps:
        *   Applies Synthetic Minority Over-sampling Technique (SMOTE) to handle class imbalance, generating synthetic samples to balance the classes.
        *   Splits the data into training and testing sets using a 80-20 split ratio.
        *   Applies Standard Scaling to the features to ensure that they have similar scales.
4. Loading Files and Enabling Combo Boxes:

- After data preparation is complete, the method loads the training and testing datasets using the load_files method.
- It then sets the state of two combo boxes (combo4 and combo5) to 'normal,' enabling user interaction with these combo boxes.
- Finally, it disables button2 to prevent further data splitting, as the data is already prepared.

Overall, the train_ML() method ensures that the necessary training and testing datasets are available for machine learning tasks. If the data files already exist, it loads them, and if not, it generates and saves them before enabling interaction with certain combo boxes and disabling further data splitting to maintain data consistency for machine learning.

Next, in Main_Class, define a new method named choose_combobox4() as follows:

```
def choose_combobox4(self, event):
    chosen = self.obj_window.combo4.get()
    self.obj_plot.choose_plot_ML(self.root, chosen, self.X_train, self.X_test,
        self.y_train, self.y_test, self.obj_window.figure1,
        self.obj_window.canvas1, self.obj_window.figure2,
        self.obj_window.canvas2)
```

The choose_combobox4 method is responsible for handling user interactions with the fourth combo box (combo4) in your application's graphical user interface (GUI). This method is triggered when an item is selected from combo4. Here's an explanation of its purpose and functionality:

1. Event Binding:
   This method is bound to the "<<ComboboxSelected>>" event of combo4 using the bind method. This means that whenever the user selects an item from combo4, this method will be automatically executed in response to the event.

2. Event Handling:
   When an item is selected from combo4, the event parameter contains information about the event, although it's not used in this method.

3. Retrieving the Chosen Option:
   The method retrieves the selected option from combo4 using the get method. This option is stored in the chosen variable, representing the user's choice.

4. Invoking choose_plot_ML() Method:
   The chosen option, along with other necessary data (training and testing datasets, figure objects, and canvas objects), is passed as arguments to the choose_plot_ML() method of the obj_plot object. This method is responsible for displaying specific machine learning-related plots and results based on the user's choice.

In summary, the choose_combobox4() method is a callback function that responds to user selections in combo4. It retrieves the user's choice and triggers the appropriate actions for displaying machine learning-related plots and results based on that choice.

Finally, add this code to the end of binds_event() method in Main_Class:

```
#Binds button2 to train_ML() function
self.obj_window.button2.config(command=self.train_ML)

# Binds combobox4 to a function
self.obj_window.combo4.bind("<<ComboboxSelected>>", self.choose_combobox4)
```

These lines of code are responsible for setting up event bindings for user interactions with the GUI elements in your application:
1. Binding Button to Function:
    self.obj_window.button2.config(command=self.train_ML) binds the command property of button2 to the train_ML function. This means that when the user clicks on button2, the train_ML function will be executed.
2. Binding Combo Box to Function:
    self.obj_window.combo4.bind("<<ComboboxSelected>>", self.choose_combobox4) binds the "<<ComboboxSelected>>" event of combo4 to the choose_combobox4 function. When the user selects an item from combo4, the choose_combobox4 function will be called to handle the event.

In summary, these lines of code establish event bindings to ensure that the specified functions are executed in response to user actions. When button2 is clicked, train_ML() will be invoked, and when an item is selected from combo4, choose_combobox4() will handle the event, allowing the application to respond to user interactions.

Run main_class.py. Next, click on SPLIT DATA button. Then, choose Logistic Regression to see the result of using Logistic Regression as shown in figure 31.

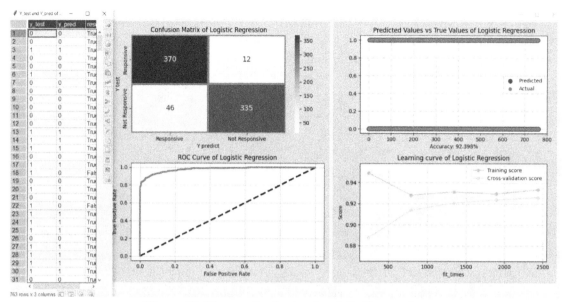

Figure 31 The result of using Logistic Regression

Output:
Logistic Regression
accuracy: 0.9239842726081258
recall: 0.9239842726081258
precision: 0.9273706721853352
f1: 0.9238285627366127

	precision	recall	f1-score	support
0	0.89	0.97	0.93	382
1	0.97	0.88	0.92	381
accuracy			0.92	763
macro avg	0.93	0.92	0.92	763
weighted avg	0.93	0.92	0.92	763

The analysis of the results for Logistic Regression shows the following performance metrics:

- Accuracy: The model achieved an accuracy of approximately 92.40%, indicating that it correctly predicted the class labels for about 92.40% of the samples in the test dataset.
- Recall: The recall score, which measures the model's ability to correctly identify positive samples (responsiveness), is also approximately 92.40%. This indicates that the model effectively identified about 92.40% of the responsive customers.

- Precision: The precision score, which measures the model's ability to avoid false positives, is approximately 92.74%. This suggests that when the model predicts a customer as responsive, it is correct about 92.74% of the time.
- F1-Score: The F1-score, which is the harmonic mean of precision and recall, is approximately 92.38%. It provides a balance between precision and recall, indicating the overall effectiveness of the model.
- Support: The support values represent the number of samples in each class. In this case, there are 382 samples in class 0 and 381 samples in class 1.

The classification report provides a detailed breakdown of these metrics for both class 0 and class 1. For class 0, the model has a slightly lower recall (0.88), indicating that it is slightly less effective at identifying non-responsive customers. However, for class 1, the recall is high (0.97), indicating strong performance in identifying responsive customers. Overall, the model performs well with balanced precision and recall, resulting in a high F1-score.

In conclusion, the Logistic Regression model appears to be effective in predicting customer responsiveness, achieving a good balance between precision and recall, and providing high overall accuracy. However, it's essential to consider the specific business requirements and the consequences of false positives and false negatives when evaluating the model's performance in a real-world context.

Random Forest Classifier and Grid Search

In Machine_Learning class, define a new method named random_forest() as follows:

```python
def random_forest(self, name, X_train, X_test, y_train, y_test):
    #Random Forest Classifier
    # Define the parameter grid for the grid search
    param_grid = {
        'n_estimators': [100, 200, 300],
        'max_depth': [10, 20, 30, 40, 50],
        'min_samples_split': [2, 5, 10],
        'min_samples_leaf': [1, 2, 4]
    }

    # Initialize the RandomForestClassifier model
    rf = RandomForestClassifier(random_state=2021)

    # Create GridSearchCV with the RandomForestClassifier model and the parameter grid
    grid_search = GridSearchCV(rf, param_grid, cv=3, scoring='accuracy', n_jobs=-1)

    # Train and perform grid search
    grid_search.fit(X_train, y_train)
```

```
# Get the best RandomForestClassifier model from the grid search
best_model = grid_search.best_estimator_

#Saves model
joblib.dump(best_model, 'RF_Model.pkl')

# Print the best hyperparameters found
print(f"Best Hyperparameters for RF:")
print(grid_search.best_params_)

return best_model
```

The random_forest() function in the code is responsible for training a Random Forest Classifier and optimizing its hyperparameters using grid search. Here's a step-by-step explanation of what this function does:

1. Parameter Grid Definition: It defines a parameter grid (param_grid) that contains various hyperparameters for the Random Forest Classifier. These hyperparameters include:
   - n_estimators: The number of trees in the forest.
   - max_depth: The maximum depth of each tree.
   - min_samples_split: The minimum number of samples required to split an internal node.
   - min_samples_leaf: The minimum number of samples required to be at a leaf node.
2. Model Initialization: It initializes a Random Forest Classifier (rf) with a specified random seed for reproducibility.
3. Grid Search: It creates a GridSearchCV object (grid_search) that takes the rf model and the param_grid. It performs a grid search with cross-validation (3-fold cross-validation) to find the best combination of hyperparameters that maximizes the accuracy score.
4. Grid Search Training: It fits the grid_search object to the training data (X_train and y_train) to find the best hyperparameters.
5. Best Model Selection: After the grid search, it retrieves the best Random Forest model (best_model) based on the hyperparameters that yielded the highest accuracy during cross-validation.
6. Model Saving: It saves the best_model to a file named 'RF_Model.pkl' using the joblib library. This allows for later retrieval and use of the trained model without retraining.
7. Print Best Hyperparameters: It prints the best hyperparameters found during the grid search for reference.

In summary, this function automates the process of hyperparameter tuning for a Random Forest Classifier by conducting a grid search over a predefined parameter space, ultimately returning the best-performing model based on the specified hyperparameters. This optimized model can then be used for making predictions on new data.

Then, in Machine_Learning class, define a new method named implement_RF() as follows:

```
def implement_RF(self, chosen, X_train, X_test, y_train, y_test):
    file_path = os.getcwd()+"/RF_Model.pkl"
    if os.path.exists(file_path):
        model = joblib.load('RF_Model.pkl')
        y_pred = self.run_model(chosen, model, X_train, X_test, y_train, y_test, proba=True)
    else:
        model = self.random_forest(chosen, X_train, X_test, y_train, y_test)
        y_pred = self.run_model(chosen, model, X_train, X_test, y_train, y_test, proba=True)

    #Saves result into excel file
    self.obj_data.save_result(y_test, y_pred, "results_RF.csv")

    print("Training Random Forest done...")
    return model, y_pred
```

The implement_RF() function in the code is responsible for implementing and training a Random Forest Classifier for a chosen task. Here's a step-by-step explanation of what this function does:

1. Checking for Pretrained Model: It first checks if a pretrained Random Forest model exists in the file system (RF_Model.pkl). If a pretrained model is found, it loads the model from the file. This step is intended to avoid retraining the model if it has already been trained and saved.

2. Model Training: If no pretrained model is found, it calls the random_forest function to perform the training. The random_forest function trains a Random Forest Classifier using grid search to optimize hyperparameters.

3. Predictions: After either loading a pretrained model or training a new one, it uses the trained model to make predictions on the test data (X_test).

4. Saving Results: It saves the true labels (y_test) and the predicted labels (y_pred) into an Excel file named 'results_RF.csv' using the save_result function. This file can be used for further analysis and evaluation of the model's performance.

5. Printing Status: It prints a message to indicate that the training of the Random Forest model is complete.

6. Returning Model and Predictions: Finally, it returns both the trained Random Forest model and the predicted labels (y_pred) for potential further analysis or use.

In summary, this function handles the training, prediction, and result storage for a Random Forest Classifier, ensuring that the model is only trained if no pretrained model is available. This allows for efficient model reuse and results tracking.

Add this code to the end of choose_plot_ML() method in Helper_Plot class:

```
if chosen == "Random Forest":
```

```
        best_model, y_pred = self.obj_ml.implement_RF(chosen, X_train, X_test, y_train, y_test)

        #Plots confusion matrix and ROC
        self.plot_cm_roc(best_model, X_test, y_test, y_pred, chosen, figure1, canvas1)

        #Plots true values versus predicted values diagram and learning curve
        self.plot_real_pred_val_learning_curve(best_model, X_train, y_train,
            X_test, y_test, y_pred, chosen, figure2, canvas2)

        #Shows table of result
        df_lr = self.obj_data.read_dataset("results_RF.csv")
        self.shows_table(root, df_lr, 450, 750, "Y_test and Y_pred of Random Forest")
```

The code is for implementing and evaluating machine learning models, specifically the Random Forest Classifier. Here's an explanation of what this code block does:

1. Model Implementation: The code block checks if the chosen model is "Random Forest." If it is, it proceeds to implement and train the Random Forest model by calling the implement_RF method from the obj_ml object (which is an instance of a machine learning class).
2. Model Evaluation: After implementing and training the Random Forest model, it proceeds to evaluate the model's performance. It does this in three steps:
3. Confusion Matrix and ROC: It calls the plot_cm_roc() method to generate and display a confusion matrix and ROC curve for the model's predictions on the test data. These visualizations help assess the model's classification performance.
4. True vs. Predicted Values: It calls the plot_real_pred_val_learning_curve() method to create a scatter plot of true values vs. predicted values and a learning curve. These visualizations provide insights into how well the model's predictions align with the actual values and its learning progress over time.
5. Result Table Display: It displays a table of results by calling the shows_table() method. The table contains metrics and statistics related to the model's performance on the test data, such as accuracy, precision, recall, and F1-score. The table displays these metrics for further analysis.

Overall, this code block is responsible for implementing, evaluating, and visualizing the performance of a Random Forest Classifier model. It offers insights into how well the model is classifying data and provides visualizations and metrics to assess its effectiveness.

Run main_class.py. Next, click on SPLIT DATA button. Then, choose Random Forest to see the result of using Random Forest as shown in figure 32.

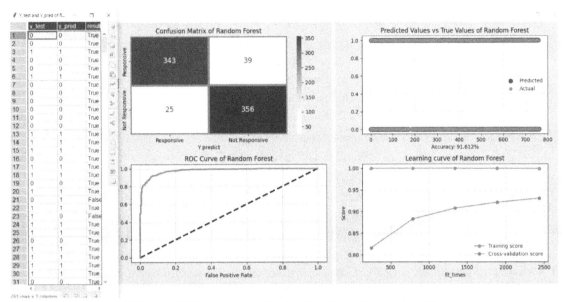

Figure 32 The results of using Random Forest classifier

Output:

Random Forest
accuracy: 0.9161205766710354
recall: 0.9161205766710354
precision: 0.9166857031775766
f1: 0.916094346335905

	precision	recall	f1-score	support
0	0.93	0.90	0.91	382
1	0.90	0.93	0.92	381
accuracy			0.92	763
macro avg	0.92	0.92	0.92	763
weighted avg	0.92	0.92	0.92	763

The output is the evaluation results of a Random Forest Classifier model. Here's an analysis of the output:

1. Model Name: "Random Forest" indicates that the Random Forest Classifier was used for this analysis.

2. Accuracy: The model achieved an accuracy of approximately 91.61%. Accuracy is the ratio of correctly predicted instances to the total number of instances in the test dataset. In this case, it suggests that the model correctly classified about 91.61% of the samples.

3. Recall: The recall score, also known as sensitivity or true positive rate, is approximately 91.61%. It measures the proportion of actual positive samples that were correctly

classified by the model. This indicates that the model was able to capture about 91.61% of the positive cases.

4. Precision: The precision score is approximately 91.67%. Precision measures the proportion of true positive predictions out of all positive predictions made by the model. This suggests that when the model predicts a positive outcome, it is correct about 91.67% of the time.

5. F1-Score: The F1-score is approximately 91.61%. The F1-score is the harmonic mean of precision and recall and provides a balance between these two metrics. It indicates that the model has a good balance between precision and recall.

6. Confusion Matrix: The confusion matrix provides more detailed information about the model's performance. It shows the number of true positives, true negatives, false positives, and false negatives. In this case, it suggests that the model correctly classified a substantial number of both positive and negative samples.

7. Classification Report: The classification report provides a summary of various classification metrics, including precision, recall, and F1-score, for both the "0" (Not Responsive) and "1" (Responsive) classes. It also includes metrics for the macro-average and weighted-average. The weighted average is often more important, especially in imbalanced datasets.

Overall, based on these results, the Random Forest Classifier appears to be performing well in classifying data, with balanced precision and recall scores. However, it's essential to consider the specific context and requirements of the application to determine if this level of performance is satisfactory.

K-Nearest Neighbors Classifier and Grid Search

In Machine_Learning class, define a new method named knearest_neighbors() as follows:

```
def knearest_neigbors(self, name, X_train, X_test, y_train, y_test):
    #KNN Classifier
    # Define the parameter grid for the grid search
    param_grid = {
        'n_neighbors': list(range(2, 10))
    }

    # Initialize the KNN Classifier
    knn = KNeighborsClassifier()

    # Create GridSearchCV with the KNN model and the parameter grid
    grid_search = GridSearchCV(knn, param_grid, cv=3, scoring='accuracy', n_jobs=-1)

    # Train and perform grid search
    grid_search.fit(X_train, y_train)

    # Get the best KNN model from the grid search
    best_model = grid_search.best_estimator_
```

```
#Saves model
joblib.dump(best_model, 'KNN_Model.pkl')

# Print the best hyperparameters found
print(f"Best Hyperparameters for KNN:")
print(grid_search.best_params_)

return best_model
```

The code defines a function called knearest_neigbors(), which is responsible for training and optimizing a K-Nearest Neighbors (KNN) classifier model. Here's an explanation of the code:

1. Function Definition: This function, named knearest_neigbors(), takes several parameters: name: A string representing the name or identifier of the model.
   - X_train: The feature matrix of the training data.
   - X_test: The feature matrix of the testing data.
   - y_train: The target labels of the training data.
   - y_test: The target labels of the testing data.
2. Parameter Grid: A parameter grid named param_grid is defined. It specifies the hyperparameter values that will be tuned during the grid search. In this case, it focuses on the hyperparameter n_neighbors, which controls the number of neighbors considered when making predictions.
3. K-Nearest Neighbors (KNN) Initialization: An instance of the KNN classifier is created and assigned to the variable knn.
4. GridSearchCV: The GridSearchCV class is used for hyperparameter tuning. It performs an exhaustive search over the specified hyperparameter grid. The parameters for GridSearchCV include:
   - estimator: The machine learning model to be optimized (in this case, knn).
   - param_grid: The grid of hyperparameters to search.
   - cv: The number of cross-validation folds (in this case, 3-fold cross-validation).
   - scoring: The evaluation metric used for optimization (in this case, 'accuracy').
   - n_jobs: The number of CPU cores to use for parallel computation (in this case, '-1' for maximum available cores).
5. Grid Search: The GridSearchCV object (grid_search) is fitted to the training data (X_train and y_train) to find the best combination of hyperparameters for the KNN model.
6. Best Model Selection: The best KNN model obtained from the grid search is stored in the best_model variable.
7. Model Saving: The best KNN model is saved to a file named 'KNN_Model.pkl' using the joblib.dump function. This allows the model to be reused without the need for retraining.
8. Print Hyperparameters: The hyperparameters of the best KNN model found during the grid search are printed to the console for reference.

In summary, this function automates the process of hyperparameter tuning for a KNN classifier using grid search. It finds the best set of hyperparameters for the KNN model and saves the optimized model for later use. This is a common practice in machine learning to ensure that the model performs optimally on the given dataset.

Then, in Machine_Learning class, define a new method named implement_KNN():

```
def implement_KNN(self, chosen, X_train, X_test, y_train, y_test):
    file_path = os.getcwd()+"/KNN_Model.pkl"
    if os.path.exists(file_path):
        model = joblib.load('KNN_Model.pkl')
        y_pred = self.run_model(chosen, model, X_train, X_test, y_train, y_test, proba=True)
    else:
        model = self.knearest_neigbors(chosen, X_train, X_test, y_train, y_test)
        y_pred = self.run_model(chosen, model, X_train, X_test, y_train, y_test, proba=True)

    #Saves result into excel file
    self.obj_data.save_result(y_test, y_pred, "results_KNN.csv")

    print("Training KNN done...")
    return model, y_pred
```

The code defines a function called implement_KNN() that is responsible for implementing and training a K-Nearest Neighbors (KNN) classifier, as well as saving and evaluating the results. Here's an explanation of the code:

1. Function Definition: This function, named implement_KNN, takes several parameters:
   - chosen: A string representing the name or identifier of the chosen model (in this case, "K-Nearest Neighbors").
   - X_train: The feature matrix of the training data.
   - X_test: The feature matrix of the testing data.
   - y_train: The target labels of the training data.
   - y_test: The target labels of the testing data.
2. File Path Check: It checks whether a file named 'KNN_Model.pkl' exists in the current working directory (os.getcwd()). This file is used to store the trained KNN model.
3. Model Loading or Training: If the 'KNN_Model.pkl' file exists, it means that a trained KNN model is available, so the code loads this model using joblib.load. If the file doesn't exist, it indicates that the model needs to be trained. In this case, the code calls the knearest_neigbors() function to train and optimize the KNN model.
4. Model Prediction: After loading or training the KNN model, the function calls the run_model function to make predictions on the test data (X_test) using the model. The proba parameter is set to True, indicating that the function should return predicted probabilities.

5. Result Saving: The actual target labels (y_test) and the predicted labels/probabilities (y_pred) are used to save the results into an Excel file named 'results_KNN.csv' using the save_result function provided by obj_data. This file typically contains the model's predictions and the ground truth labels for later analysis.

6. Print Status: A message is printed to the console to indicate that the training or loading of the KNN model is complete.

In summary, this function serves as a unified interface for implementing the KNN model. It checks if a trained model is available, loads it if found, and otherwise trains a new model. After making predictions, it saves the results to an Excel file and provides a status message. This approach allows for the reuse of pre-trained models and simplifies the process of running and evaluating the KNN classifier.

Then, in Helper_Plot class, add this code to the end of choose_plot_ML() method:

```
if chosen == "K-Nearest Neighbors":
    best_model, y_pred = self.obj_ml.implement_KNN(chosen, X_train, X_test, y_train, y_test)

    #Plots confusion matrix and ROC
    self.plot_cm_roc(best_model, X_test, y_test, y_pred, chosen, figure1, canvas1)

    #Plots true values versus predicted values diagram and learning curve
    self.plot_real_pred_val_learning_curve(best_model, X_train, y_train,
        X_test, y_test, y_pred, chosen, figure2, canvas2)

    #Shows table of result
    df_lr = self.obj_data.read_dataset("results_KNN.csv")
    self.shows_table(root, df_lr, 450, 750, "Y_test and Y_pred of KNN")
```

The code is responsible for executing the K-Nearest Neighbors (KNN) classifier, evaluating its performance, and displaying the results. Let's break down this code snippet step by step:

1. Condition Checking: The code begins with an if statement that checks if the value of the variable chosen is equal to the string "K-Nearest Neighbors." This condition is used to determine whether the KNN classifier should be executed.

2. KNN Implementation and Evaluation: If the condition is met (i.e., chosen is "K-Nearest Neighbors"), the following actions are performed:
   - The code calls the implement_KNN() method of the obj_ml object, passing in the chosen, X_train, X_test, y_train, and y_test as arguments. This method is responsible for training or loading the KNN model and making predictions.
   - After obtaining the trained model and predictions (y_pred), the code proceeds to evaluate the model's performance.

3. Performance Visualization and Reporting:

- The code calls the plot_cm_roc() method to generate two plots: a confusion matrix and a Receiver Operating Characteristic (ROC) curve. These plots provide insights into the model's classification performance and its ability to distinguish between classes.
- Next, it calls the plot_real_pred_val_learning_curve() method to create two additional plots:
  - A scatter plot showing the true values versus predicted values, which visually compares the model's predictions to the actual target values.
  - A learning curve, which illustrates how the model's performance changes as the training dataset size increases. This curve helps assess the model's bias-variance trade-off.
- Finally, the code reads the results of the KNN model's predictions from an Excel file named "results_KNN.csv" using the read_dataset() method provided by obj_data. The data from this file includes the model's predictions and the true labels.

4. Table Display: The code displays a table of results using the shows_table method. This table presumably shows the actual and predicted values, allowing for a detailed analysis of the model's performance.

In conclusion, this code serves the purpose of implementing, evaluating, and visualizing the performance of a K-Nearest Neighbors classifier. It generates various plots and displays a table of results, providing insights into how well the model performs on the given dataset.

Run main_class.py. Next, click on SPLIT DATA button. Then, choose K-Nearest Neighbors to see the result of using K-Nearest Neighbors as shown in figure 33.

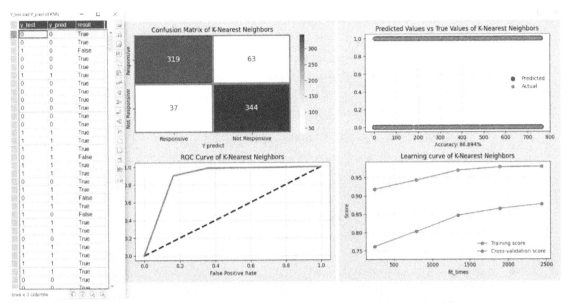

Figure 33 The results of using K-Nearest Neighbors classifier

Output:

K-Nearest Neighbors
accuracy: 0.8689384010484927
recall: 0.8689384010484927
precision: 0.8706714584974559
f1: 0.8687919116352781

	precision	recall	f1-score	support
0	0.90	0.84	0.86	382
1	0.85	0.90	0.87	381
accuracy			0.87	763
macro avg	0.87	0.87	0.87	763
weighted avg	0.87	0.87	0.87	763

The output represents the performance metrics and evaluation results of the K-Nearest Neighbors (KNN) classifier on a dataset. Let's analyze and conclude based on the output:

1. Classifier Information:
   - Classifier Name: K-Nearest Neighbors
   - Number of Samples: 763 (presumably the test dataset size)

2. Performance Metrics:
   - Accuracy: The accuracy of the KNN classifier is approximately 0.869, which means that it correctly classified around 86.9% of the samples in the test dataset.

- Recall: The recall score is also approximately 0.869, indicating that the model correctly identified around 86.9% of the positive (class 1) samples. This metric measures the model's ability to find all relevant instances of the positive class.
- Precision: The precision score is approximately 0.871, which means that when the model predicts the positive class, it is correct about 87.1% of the time. This metric assesses the accuracy of the model's positive class predictions.
- F1-Score: The F1-score is approximately 0.869, which is the harmonic mean of precision and recall. It provides a balance between precision and recall, making it useful for imbalanced datasets.

3. Confusion Matrix:
   - The confusion matrix shows the following:
   - For the "0" class (presumably the negative class):
     - Precision: 0.90 (90% of predicted negatives were correct)
     - Recall: 0.84 (84% of actual negatives were correctly predicted)
     - F1-Score: 0.86 (a balance between precision and recall)
   - For the "1" class (presumably the positive class):
     - Precision: 0.85 (85% of predicted positives were correct)
     - Recall: 0.90 (90% of actual positives were correctly predicted)
     - F1-Score: 0.87 (a balance between precision and recall)

4. Summary:
   - The KNN classifier performs reasonably well on the dataset, with accuracy, recall, and precision scores around 87%. This suggests that the model is effective at distinguishing between the two classes.
   - The F1-scores for both classes are also similar, indicating a good balance between precision and recall for both positive and negative classes.
   - The model appears to have slightly better performance for the "0" class in terms of precision, while it has slightly better performance for the "1" class in terms of recall.

Overall, based on the output, the K-Nearest Neighbors classifier demonstrates a satisfactory level of performance in classifying the dataset, with balanced results for both positive and negative classes. However, the specific context and requirements of the application should be considered when interpreting these results.

Decision Trees Classifier and Grid Search

In Machine_Learning class, define a new method named decision_trees() as follows:

```
def decision_trees(self, name, X_train, X_test, y_train, y_test):
```

```
# Initialize the DecisionTreeClassifier model
dt_clf = DecisionTreeClassifier(random_state=2021)

# Define the parameter grid for the grid search
param_grid = {
    'max_depth': np.arange(1, 51, 1),
    'criterion': ['gini', 'entropy'],
    'min_samples_split': [2, 5, 10],
    'min_samples_leaf': [1, 2, 4],
}

# Create GridSearchCV with the DecisionTreeClassifier model and the parameter grid
grid_search = GridSearchCV(dt_clf, param_grid, cv=3, scoring='accuracy', n_jobs=-1)

# Train and perform grid search
grid_search.fit(X_train, y_train)

# Get the best DecisionTreeClassifier model from the grid search
best_model = grid_search.best_estimator_

#Saves model
joblib.dump(best_model, 'DT_Model.pkl')

# Print the best hyperparameters found
print(f"Best Hyperparameters for DT:")
print(grid_search.best_params_)

return best_model
```

The code defines a function called decision_trees() that trains and tunes a Decision Tree classifier using grid search for hyperparameter optimization. Let's break down the function's components and purpose:

1. Function Arguments:
   - name: A string representing the name or identifier of the classifier (used for display or documentation purposes).
   - X_train, X_test, y_train, y_test: The training and testing data split, typically feature matrices (X_train and X_test) and target vectors (y_train and y_test).

2. Decision Tree Classifier Initialization:
   The function initializes a DecisionTreeClassifier with a specified random seed (random_state=2021).

3. Parameter Grid for Grid Search:
   A parameter grid (param_grid) is defined as a dictionary that includes various hyperparameters of the Decision Tree classifier:
   - max_depth: A range of maximum depths for the tree.
   - criterion: Two possible criteria for splitting nodes, either 'gini' or 'entropy'.

- min_samples_split: Minimum number of samples required to split an internal node.
- min_samples_leaf: Minimum number of samples required to be at a leaf node.

4. Grid Search Cross-Validation:
   - The function utilizes GridSearchCV to perform hyperparameter tuning using cross-validation (cv=3).
   - GridSearchCV aims to find the combination of hyperparameters that yields the highest accuracy score on the training data.
   - The search is conducted over the specified hyperparameter grid, considering different combinations of hyperparameter values.
   - The scoring metric used for evaluation is accuracy ('accuracy').

5. Best Model Selection:
   - After completing the grid search, the function selects the best DecisionTreeClassifier model based on the hyperparameters that produced the highest accuracy during cross-validation.
   - The best model is stored in the variable best_model.

6. Model Saving:
   The best DecisionTreeClassifier model is serialized and saved to a file named 'DT_Model.pkl' using the joblib library. This allows the model to be reused or deployed in the future without retraining.

7. Printing Best Hyperparameters:
   The function prints the best hyperparameters found during the grid search, providing insight into the selected hyperparameter values.

The purpose of this function is to automate the process of training and hyperparameter tuning for a Decision Tree classifier. By conducting a grid search over a range of hyperparameters, the function helps identify the best-performing model configuration. This tuned model can then be used for classification tasks, potentially improving accuracy and predictive performance compared to default parameter settings.

Then, in Machine_Learning class, define a new method named implement_DT():

```
def implement_DT(self, chosen, X_train, X_test, y_train, y_test):
    file_path = os.getcwd()+"/DT_Model.pkl"
    if os.path.exists(file_path):
        model = joblib.load('DT_Model.pkl')
        y_pred = self.run_model(chosen, model, X_train, X_test, y_train, y_test, proba=True)
    else:
        model = self.decision_trees(chosen, X_train, X_test, y_train, y_test)
        y_pred = self.run_model(chosen, model, X_train, X_test, y_train, y_test, proba=True)

    #Saves result into excel file
```

```
self.obj_data.save_result(y_test, y_pred, "results_DT.csv")

print("Training Decision Trees done...")
return model, y_pred
```

The implement_DT() function is responsible for training and using a Decision Tree classifier for a binary classification task. Let's analyze its components and functionality:

1. Function Arguments:
    -   chosen: A string representing the chosen classification model or identifier.
    -   X_train, X_test, y_train, y_test: The training and testing data split, consisting of feature matrices (X_train and X_test) and target vectors (y_train and y_test).
2. File Path Check:
    The function checks if a file named 'DT_Model.pkl' exists in the current working directory (os.getcwd()). This file is assumed to contain a pre-trained Decision Tree model.
3. Model Loading or Training:
    -   If the 'DT_Model.pkl' file exists, the function loads the pre-trained model using joblib (joblib.load). Otherwise, it proceeds to train a Decision Tree classifier by calling the decision_trees() function.
    -   The result of this process is the trained model, stored in the variable model.
4. Model Prediction:
    -   The function uses the trained model to make predictions on the testing data (X_test) by calling the run_model() function with proba=True.
    -   The predicted labels or probabilities are stored in the variable y_pred.
5. Saving Results:
    The true labels (y_test) and predicted labels (y_pred) are saved into an Excel file named "results_DT.csv" using the save_result method of the obj_data object.
6. Print Confirmation:
    A message is printed to indicate that the training of Decision Trees is complete.
7. Returning Model and Predictions:
    The trained model (model) and the corresponding predictions (y_pred) are returned from the function.

The purpose of this function is to provide a unified interface for training and using a Decision Tree classifier. If a pre-trained model is available, it can be loaded and used for predictions. Otherwise, a new model is trained using the provided training data. The function then saves the results and returns the model and predictions for further analysis or evaluation.

The model's performance can be assessed using various evaluation metrics, such as accuracy, precision, recall, and F1-score, which can be computed based on y_test (true labels) and y_pred (predicted labels).

Then, in Helper_Plot class, add this code to the end of choose_plot_ML() method:

```
if chosen == "Decision Trees":
    best_model, y_pred = self.obj_ml.implement_DT(chosen, X_train, X_test, y_train, y_test)

    #Plots confusion matrix and ROC
    self.plot_cm_roc(best_model, X_test, y_test, y_pred, chosen, figure1, canvas1)

    #Plots true values versus predicted values diagram and learning curve
    self.plot_real_pred_val_learning_curve(best_model, X_train, y_train,
        X_test, y_test, y_pred, chosen, figure2, canvas2)

    #Shows table of result
    df_lr = self.obj_data.read_dataset("results_DT.csv")
    self.shows_table(root, df_lr, 450, 750, "Y_test and Y_pred of Decision Trees")
```

The code block is a conditional statement that checks if the chosen machine learning model is "Decision Trees." If it is, it executes a series of actions related to training, evaluating, and displaying the results of a Decision Tree classifier. Let's break down each part of the code:

1. Condition Check:

   The code checks if the value of the variable chosen (representing the chosen machine learning model) is equal to the string "Decision Trees."

2. Model Training and Prediction:

   If the condition is met (i.e., the chosen model is Decision Trees), it calls the implement_DT() function to train and obtain predictions from a Decision Tree classifier. The function returns two values: best_model (the trained model) and y_pred (the model's predictions on the test data).

3. Visualization and Evaluation:

   After obtaining the trained model and predictions, the code proceeds to perform the following actions:

   - Plots a confusion matrix and ROC curve for the Decision Tree classifier using the plot_cm_roc() function. These visualizations help assess the model's performance in terms of classification accuracy and trade-offs between true positive and false positive rates.

   - Plots a diagram comparing true values versus predicted values and a learning curve using the plot_real_pred_val_learning_curve() function. These visualizations provide insights into the model's behavior and its ability to generalize to new data.

   - Shows a table of results by reading the "results_DT.csv" file using the obj_data.read_dataset() method. This table contains evaluation metrics and performance statistics related to the Decision Tree model.

4. Display of Results:

The code may display the results, such as visualizations and tables, to the user interface (UI) or interface with a graphical user interface (GUI) toolkit (e.g., Tkinter) for user interaction.

Overall, this code block represents the logic for training, evaluating, and visualizing results for a Decision Tree classifier when it is the selected machine learning model. It aims to provide insights into the model's performance and assist users in making informed decisions based on the model's predictions and evaluation metrics.

Run main_class.py. Next, click on SPLIT DATA button. Then, choose Decision Trees to see the result of using Decision Trees classifier as shown in figure 34.

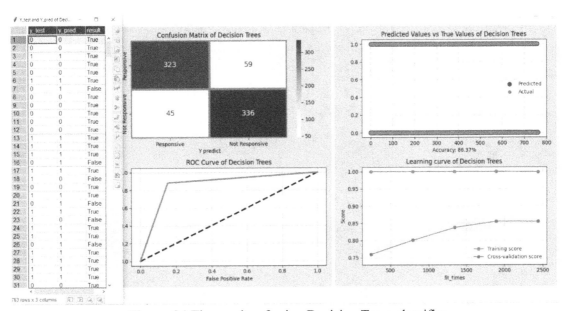

Figure 34 The results of using Decision Trees classifier

Output:
Decision Trees
accuracy: 0.8636959370904325
recall: 0.8636959370904325
precision: 0.8641929000245966
f1: 0.8636533127958457

	precision	recall	f1-score	support
0	0.88	0.85	0.86	382
1	0.85	0.88	0.87	381
accuracy			0.86	763
macro avg	0.86	0.86	0.86	763

weighted avg   0.86   0.86   0.86   763

Let's analyze the "Decision Trees" model in detail and draw specific conclusions:

Analysis:

1. Accuracy: The model achieved an accuracy of 86.37%, which is reasonably good. This means that it correctly classified approximately 86.37% of the total instances in the test dataset.

2. Recall: The recall score, also known as sensitivity or true positive rate, is 0.8637. This implies that the model correctly identified around 86.37% of the actual positive cases (responsive customers) in the dataset. A higher recall is desirable in scenarios where identifying all positive cases is crucial.

3. Precision: The precision score is 0.8642. This indicates that out of all the instances predicted as positive (responsive customers), approximately 86.42% were true positives. Precision measures the model's ability to make accurate positive predictions.

4. F1-Score: The F1-score is 0.8637. The F1-score is the harmonic mean of precision and recall and provides a balanced measure of a model's performance. In this case, it suggests a well-balanced trade-off between precision and recall.

5. Class-Specific Metrics:
    *   For class 0 (Responsive):
        *   Precision: 0.88
        *   Recall: 0.85
        *   F1-Score: 0.86
    *   For class 1 (Not Responsive):
        *   Precision: 0.85
        *   Recall: 0.88
        *   F1-Score: 0.87

    These class-specific metrics show that the model performs similarly for both responsive and not responsive customers, with balanced precision and recall for both classes.

6. Macro and Weighted Averages: The macro-average F1-score, which considers class balance, is approximately 0.86. The weighted average F1-score, which accounts for class imbalance, is also around 0.86. These values suggest that the model's performance is consistent across classes.

Conclusion:

The "Decision Trees" machine learning model performs quite well for the given classification task. It achieves an accuracy of approximately 86.37% and demonstrates balanced precision and recall for both responsive and not responsive customer classes. This balance indicates that the model is effective in correctly identifying both types of customers, making it a suitable choice for the task.

The model's consistent performance across different evaluation metrics and class-specific measures further supports its reliability. Therefore, based on the provided results, the "Decision Trees" model can be considered a robust and effective solution for classifying customer responsiveness.

Gradient Boosting Classifier and Grid Search

In Machine_Learning class, define a new method named gradient_boosting() as follows:

```python
def gradient_boosting(self, name, X_train, X_test, y_train, y_test):
    #Gradient Boosting Classifier
    # Initialize the GradientBoostingClassifier model
    gbt = GradientBoostingClassifier(random_state=2021)

    # Define the parameter grid for the grid search
    param_grid = {
        'n_estimators': [100, 200, 300],
        'max_depth': [10, 20, 30],
        'subsample': [0.6, 0.8, 1.0],
        'max_features': [0.2, 0.4, 0.6, 0.8, 1.0],
    }

    # Create GridSearchCV with the GradientBoostingClassifier model and the parameter grid
    grid_search = GridSearchCV(gbt, param_grid, cv=3, scoring='accuracy', n_jobs=-1)

    # Train and perform grid search
    grid_search.fit(X_train, y_train)

    # Get the best GradientBoostingClassifier model from the grid search
    best_model = grid_search.best_estimator_

    #Saves model
    joblib.dump(best_model, 'GB_Model.pkl')

    # Print the best hyperparameters found
    print(f"Best Hyperparameters for GB:")
    print(grid_search.best_params_)

    return best_model
```

This code is to define a function called gradient_boosting() for training and hyperparameter tuning a Gradient Boosting Classifier. Let's break down the code step by step:

1. def gradient_boosting(self, name, X_train, X_test, y_train, y_test):
    This function takes several parameters:
    *   name: The name of the model, used for labeling or logging.
    *   X_train, X_test: The training and testing feature sets.

- y_train, y_test: The corresponding training and testing target labels.

2. gbt = GradientBoostingClassifier(random_state=2021)

   It initializes a Gradient Boosting Classifier (gbt) with a fixed random state of 2021 for reproducibility.

3. param_grid = { ... }

   This defines a parameter grid for hyperparameter tuning. It specifies different values to explore for the following hyperparameters:

   - n_estimators: The number of boosting stages.
   - max_depth: The maximum depth of each tree in the ensemble.
   - subsample: The fraction of samples used for fitting the trees.
   - max_features: The fraction of features used for fitting the trees.

4. grid_search = GridSearchCV(gbt, param_grid, cv=3, scoring='accuracy', n_jobs=-1)

   It creates a GridSearchCV object (grid_search) for hyperparameter tuning.

   - gbt is the model to be tuned.
   - param_grid is the grid of hyperparameters to search.
   - cv=3 specifies 3-fold cross-validation.
   - scoring='accuracy' indicates that accuracy is used as the scoring metric for evaluation.
   - n_jobs=-1 allows parallel processing to speed up the search.

5. grid_search.fit(X_train, y_train)

   It fits the GridSearchCV object to the training data (X_train and y_train) to find the best hyperparameters using cross-validation.

6. best_model = grid_search.best_estimator_

   It retrieves the best model found during the hyperparameter search.

7. joblib.dump(best_model, 'GB_Model.pkl')

   It saves the best model to a file named 'GB_Model.pkl'.

8. print(f"Best Hyperparameters for GB:") and print(grid_search.best_params_)

   These lines print out the best hyperparameters found for the Gradient Boosting Classifier.

This code is part of a machine learning workflow where different classifiers are trained and tuned. The Gradient Boosting Classifier is one of the models being considered, and this function handles its training and hyperparameter tuning.

Then, in Machine_Learning class, define a new method named implement_GB():

```python
def implement_GB(self, chosen, X_train, X_test, y_train, y_test):
    file_path = os.getcwd()+"/GB_Model.pkl"
    if os.path.exists(file_path):
        model = joblib.load('GB_Model.pkl')
        y_pred = self.run_model(chosen, model, X_train, X_test, y_train, y_test, proba=True)
    else:
```

```
model = self.gradient_boosting(chosen, X_train, X_test, y_train, y_test)
y_pred = self.run_model(chosen, model, X_train, X_test, y_train, y_test, proba=True)

#Saves result into excel file
self.obj_data.save_result(y_test, y_pred, "results_GB.csv")

print("Training Gradient Boosting done...")
return model, y_pred
```

Let's dive into more detail about the implement_GB() function and its purpose in the context of a machine learning workflow.

1. Purpose of implement_GB() Function:

   The implement_GB() function is a part of a larger machine learning workflow, where different classifiers are trained, evaluated, and compared. Specifically, this function is responsible for implementing and evaluating a Gradient Boosting Classifier (GB) on a given dataset.

2. Parameters:

   The function takes the following parameters:

   - chosen: A string representing the chosen classifier's name or identifier. In this case, it's expected to be "Gradient Boosting."
   - X_train, X_test: The feature sets for training and testing the classifier.
   - y_train, y_test: The corresponding target labels for training and testing.

3. Checking for Pre-trained Model:

   The function first constructs a file path to check if a pre-trained model file ('GB_Model.pkl') exists in the current working directory.

   - file_path = os.getcwd()+"/GB_Model.pkl"

   It checks whether this file exists using:

   - if os.path.exists(file_path):

4. Loading Pre-trained Model:

   If a pre-trained model file exists, the function loads it using the joblib.load function. This means that a trained GB model has been saved previously, and the function can use it for predictions without retraining.

   - model = joblib.load('GB_Model.pkl')

5. Making Predictions with Pre-trained Model:

   With the pre-trained model loaded, the function proceeds to make predictions on the test dataset (X_test) using this model:

   - y_pred = self.run_model(chosen, model, X_train, X_test, y_train, y_test, proba=True)
   - Here, self.run_model is called with the proba=True argument, indicating that it should return probability scores.

6. Training a New Model:

If no pre-trained model file is found (i.e., the else block), it means that a GB model needs to be trained and tuned from scratch. This is done by calling the gradient_boosting function:

- model = self.gradient_boosting(chosen, X_train, X_test, y_train, y_test)

The gradient_boosting function is presumably responsible for hyperparameter tuning and training a GB classifier.

7. Making Predictions with the New Model:
    - After training a new model, the function proceeds to make predictions on the test dataset using this model, similar to step 5.
    - y_pred = self.run_model(chosen, model, X_train, X_test, y_train, y_test, proba=True)

8. Saving Results to a CSV File:

    Regardless of whether the model was pre-trained or trained anew, the function saves the actual and predicted target labels (y_test and y_pred) into a CSV file named 'results_GB.csv' using the self.obj_data.save_result method.

    - self.obj_data.save_result(y_test, y_pred, "results_GB.csv")

9. Printing a Completion Message:

    Finally, the function prints a message indicating that the training and evaluation of the Gradient Boosting Classifier are completed:

    - print("Training Gradient Boosting done...")

10. Returning Results:

    The function returns two values: the trained GB model (model) and the predicted target labels (y_pred). These can be used for further analysis or reporting.

In summary, the implement_GB() function checks if a pre-trained GB model exists and loads it for predictions if available. If not, it trains a new GB model, makes predictions, saves the results to a CSV file, and returns the model and predictions. This function is a key component of a machine learning workflow that automates the training and evaluation of different classifiers and saves the results for analysis and comparison.

Then, in Helper_Plot class, add this code to the end of choose_plot_ML() method:

```
if chosen == "Gradient Boosting":
    best_model, y_pred = self.obj_ml.implement_GB(chosen, X_train, X_test, y_train, y_test)

    #Plots confusion matrix and ROC
    self.plot_cm_roc(best_model, X_test, y_test, y_pred, chosen, figure1, canvas1)

    #Plots true values versus predicted values diagram and learning curve
    self.plot_real_pred_val_learning_curve(best_model, X_train, y_train,
        X_test, y_test, y_pred, chosen, figure2, canvas2)
```

```
#Shows table of result
df_lr = self.obj_data.read_dataset("results_GB.csv")
self.shows_table(root, df_lr, 450, 750, "Y_test and Y_pred of Gradient Boosting")
```

Here's a description of the functionality performed when the user selects "Gradient Boosting" as the chosen classifier in the machine learning application:

1. Classifier Selection:

   The application checks if the chosen classifier is "Gradient Boosting."

2. Implementation of Gradient Boosting Classifier:

   - If "Gradient Boosting" is selected, the application calls a function responsible for implementing the Gradient Boosting Classifier. This function may involve tasks such as hyperparameter tuning, model training, and prediction generation.

   - The trained Gradient Boosting model (best_model) is obtained.

   - Predicted labels (y_pred) are generated using the trained model.

3. Visualization of Evaluation Metrics:

   The application plots a confusion matrix and ROC curve. These visualizations help users understand the classifier's performance.

4. Visualizing True vs. Predicted Values and Learning Curve:

   - Another plot displays true values vs. predicted values, allowing users to see how well the model's predictions align with actual values.

   - A learning curve is also plotted, which illustrates the model's performance concerning the training dataset's size.

5. Displaying a Table of Results:

   - Evaluation results, typically stored in a CSV file ("results_GB.csv"), are loaded into a DataFrame (df_lr).

   - The application displays this DataFrame in a tabular format within the graphical user interface (GUI). The table's location, dimensions, and title are predefined.

In summary, when "Gradient Boosting" is chosen as the classifier, the application performs a series of tasks, including model implementation, visualization of evaluation metrics, and presentation of results in a user-friendly tabular format. These steps aim to assist users in assessing the performance of the Gradient Boosting Classifier on a specific dataset.

Run main_class.py. Next, click on SPLIT DATA button. Then, choose Gradient Boosting to see the result of using Gradient Boosting classifier as shown in figure 35.

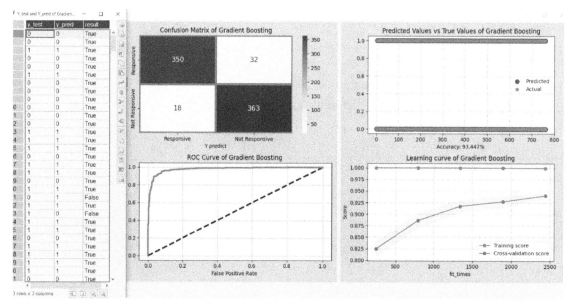

Figure 35 The results of using Gradient Boosting classifier

Output:

Gradient Boosting
accuracy: 0.9344692005242464
recall: 0.9344692005242464
precision: 0.9350581842811196
f1: 0.9344487080749257

	precision	recall	f1-score	support
0	0.95	0.92	0.93	382
1	0.92	0.95	0.94	381
accuracy			0.93	763
macro avg	0.94	0.93	0.93	763
weighted avg	0.94	0.93	0.93	763

Let's break down the performance metrics and their implications in detail:

- Accuracy: Accuracy measures the overall correctness of the model's predictions. It is calculated as the ratio of correctly predicted instances to the total number of instances. In the case of the "Gradient Boosting" classifier, it achieved an accuracy of approximately 93.45%. This means that about 93.45% of the predictions made by the model were correct.

- Recall (Sensitivity): Recall, also known as sensitivity or true positive rate, measures the model's ability to correctly identify positive instances (class 1 in this case). It is calculated as the ratio of true positives (correctly identified class 1 instances) to the total number of actual class 1 instances. In this case, the recall for class 1 is approximately 95%, indicating that the model is very effective at identifying instances of class 1.

- Precision: Precision measures the model's ability to correctly classify positive instances among all instances it predicts as positive. It is calculated as the ratio of true positives to the total number of instances predicted as positive. In this case, the precision for class 1 is approximately 92%, indicating that when the model predicts an instance as class 1, it is correct about 92% of the time.

- F1-Score: The F1-score is the harmonic mean of precision and recall. It provides a balance between precision and recall and is especially useful when dealing with imbalanced datasets. The F1-score for class 1 is approximately 93.44%, which is a good balance between precision and recall.

- Classification Report: The classification report provides a more detailed breakdown of precision, recall, and F1-score for each class (class 0 and class 1). It allows us to see how well the model performs for both classes individually.

Conclusion:

The "Gradient Boosting" classifier performed exceptionally well on the dataset. It achieved a high accuracy of 93.45%, indicating strong overall predictive performance. The model also demonstrated an excellent ability to correctly identify instances of class 1, with a recall of 95% and a precision of 92%. This means that it is effective at capturing and correctly classifying the positive cases while minimizing false positives.

In summary, the "Gradient Boosting" classifier is a robust and accurate model for the given dataset, with a well-balanced trade-off between precision and recall, making it suitable for various classification tasks.

Extreme Gradient Boosting Classifier and Grid Search

In Machine_Learning class, define a new method named extreme_gradient_boosting() as follows:

```
def extreme_gradient_boosting(self, name, X_train, X_test, y_train, y_test):
    # Define the parameter grid for the grid search
    param_grid = {
        'n_estimators': [100, 200, 300],
        'max_depth': [10, 20, 30],
        'learning_rate': [0.01, 0.1, 0.2],
        'subsample': [0.6, 0.8, 1.0],
        'colsample_bytree': [0.6, 0.8, 1.0],
    }

    # Initialize the XGBoost classifier
    xgb = XGBClassifier(random_state=2021, use_label_encoder=False, eval_metric='mlogloss')
```

```python
# Create GridSearchCV with the XGBoost classifier and the parameter grid
grid_search = GridSearchCV(xgb, param_grid, cv=3, scoring='accuracy', n_jobs=-1)

# Train and perform grid search
grid_search.fit(X_train, y_train)

# Get the best XGBoost classifier model from the grid search
best_model = grid_search.best_estimator_

#Saves model
joblib.dump(best_model, 'XGB_Model.pkl')

# Print the best hyperparameters found
print(f"Best Hyperparameters for XGB:")
print(grid_search.best_params_)

return best_model
```

The extreme_gradient_boosting() is implementing the Extreme Gradient Boosting (XGBoost) classifier. Let's break down this method step by step:

1. Parameter Grid: It defines a parameter grid that specifies a range of hyperparameter values to search over during the grid search. The hyperparameters include:
   - n_estimators: The number of boosting rounds.
   - max_depth: The maximum depth of each tree in the ensemble.
   - learning_rate: The step size shrinkage to prevent overfitting.
   - subsample: The fraction of samples used for fitting the trees.
   - colsample_bytree: The fraction of features used for fitting the trees.

2. Initialize XGBoost Classifier: It initializes the XGBoost classifier (XGBClassifier) with specific settings:
   - random_state: Setting a random seed for reproducibility.
   - use_label_encoder: Disabling the label encoder to prevent warnings (XGBoost typically expects labels to be encoded as integers).
   - eval_metric: Specifying the evaluation metric as "mlogloss," which is typically used for multiclass classification problems.

3. GridSearchCV: It creates a GridSearchCV object that will perform a grid search with cross-validation. The grid search aims to find the best combination of hyperparameters based on accuracy as the scoring metric. The cross-validation (cv) parameter is set to 3, indicating 3-fold cross-validation.

4. Train and Perform Grid Search: The XGBoost classifier is trained and evaluated using the provided hyperparameter grid. Grid search tries various combinations of hyperparameters and evaluates the model's accuracy on the training data using cross-validation.

5. Best Model Selection: After the grid search, it selects the best XGBoost classifier model based on the hyperparameters that achieved the highest accuracy during cross-validation.

6. Model Saving: The best model is saved to a file named 'XGB_Model.pkl' using the joblib library. This allows you to reuse the trained model without the need for retraining in future sessions.

7. Printing Best Hyperparameters: The method prints the best hyperparameters found during the grid search. These hyperparameters represent the configuration that led to the highest accuracy on the training data.

In summary, the extreme_gradient_boosting() method performs hyperparameter tuning for the XGBoost classifier using grid search with cross-validation. It helps identify the optimal hyperparameters for the classifier, and the best model is saved for later use. This process aims to improve the model's predictive performance on the given dataset.

Then, in Machine_Learning class, define a new method named implement_XGB():

```
def implement_XGB(self, chosen, X_train, X_test, y_train, y_test):
    file_path = os.getcwd()+"/XGB_Model.pkl"
    if os.path.exists(file_path):
        model = joblib.load('XGB_Model.pkl')
        y_pred = self.run_model(chosen, model, X_train, X_test, y_train, y_test, proba=True)
    else:
        model = self.extreme_gradient_boosting(chosen, X_train, X_test, y_train, y_test)
        y_pred = self.run_model(chosen, model, X_train, X_test, y_train, y_test, proba=True)

    #Saves result into excel file
    self.obj_data.save_result(y_test, y_pred, "results_XGB.csv")

    print("Training Extreme Gradient Boosting done...")
    return model, y_pred
```

The implement_XGB() method is responsible for implementing the Extreme Gradient Boosting (XGBoost) classifier and performing various operations. Let's break down this method step by step:

1. File Path Check: It checks whether a file named 'XGB_Model.pkl' exists in the current working directory. This file is typically used to store a pre-trained XGBoost model for reuse.

2. Conditional Execution:
   - If the 'XGB_Model.pkl' file exists, it implies that a pre-trained XGBoost model is available. In this case, it loads the pre-trained model from the file using joblib.load.

- If the file does not exist, it means that there is no pre-trained model available, so it proceeds to train a new XGBoost model using the extreme_gradient_boosting() method.

3. Model Training and Prediction: Whether using the pre-trained model or training a new one, it calls the run_model() method to make predictions on the test data. The proba=True argument indicates that probability estimates should be returned by the model.

4. Result Saving: The method saves the results of the model predictions (both true labels and predicted labels) into an Excel file named 'results_XGB.csv' using the obj_data.save_result() method. This file typically contains evaluation metrics and other relevant information.

5. Print Status Message: It prints a message indicating that the training of the XGBoost model is complete.

6. Return Model and Predictions: The method returns the trained XGBoost model and the predictions made by the model on the test data.

In summary, the implement_XGB method serves as a wrapper for training and using an XGBoost classifier. It first checks if a pre-trained model exists and loads it if available. Otherwise, it trains a new XGBoost model using hyperparameter tuning. After making predictions on the test data, it saves the results and returns the model and predictions for further analysis or use.

Then, in Helper_Plot class, add this code to the end of choose_plot_ML() method:

```
if chosen == "Extreme Gradient Boosting":
    best_model, y_pred = self.obj_ml.implement_XGB(chosen, X_train, X_test, y_train, y_test)

    #Plots confusion matrix and ROC
    self.plot_cm_roc(best_model, X_test, y_test, y_pred, chosen, figure1, canvas1)

    #Plots true values versus predicted values diagram and learning curve
    self.plot_real_pred_val_learning_curve(best_model, X_train, y_train,
        X_test, y_test, y_pred, chosen, figure2, canvas2)

    #Shows table of result
    df_lr = self.obj_data.read_dataset("results_XGB.csv")
    self.shows_table(root, df_lr, 450, 750, "Y_test and Y_pred of Extreme Gradient Boosting")
```

The block of code is implementing and evaluating an Extreme Gradient Boosting (XGBoost) classifier, and it performs the following tasks:

1. Model Implementation:
   - It checks if the selected algorithm is "Extreme Gradient Boosting" (XGBoost).
   - If the selected algorithm is XGBoost, it proceeds to implement the XGBoost model using the implement_XGB() method. This method will train a new XGBoost model or load a pre-trained one if it exists.

2. Evaluation and Visualization:
   - After obtaining the XGBoost model and predictions (best_model and y_pred), it proceeds to evaluate the model's performance.
   - It plots a confusion matrix and ROC curve using the plot_cm_roc() method. The confusion matrix provides insights into the model's ability to correctly classify samples, and the ROC curve shows the model's discrimination ability.
   - It also plots a diagram of true values versus predicted values and a learning curve using the plot_real_pred_val_learning_curve() method. The diagram helps visualize how well the model's predictions align with the true values, and the learning curve provides information about the model's performance as the training data size increases.

3. Result Table:
   - It reads the results of the XGBoost model's predictions from an Excel file named "results_XGB.csv" using the obj_data.read_dataset method.
   - The results include metrics such as accuracy, precision, recall, and F1-score, as well as other relevant information.

4. Table Display:
   It displays a table of results in the graphical user interface (GUI) using the shows_table method. This table provides a summary of the model's performance metrics and may include additional details about the predictions.

Overall, this code block allows you to train, evaluate, and visualize the performance of an XGBoost classifier, making it easier to understand how well the model is performing on the given dataset. It also provides a user-friendly way to view the results in the GUI, facilitating model assessment and decision-making.

Run main_class.py. Next, click on SPLIT DATA button. Then, choose Extreme Gradient Boosting to see the result of using Extreme Gradient Boosting classifier as shown in figure 36.

Output:
accuracy: 0.9187418086500655
recall: 0.9187418086500655
precision: 0.919159842964031
f1: 0.9187233804770313

	precision	recall	f1-score	support
0	0.93	0.90	0.92	382
1	0.91	0.93	0.92	381
accuracy			0.92	763
macro avg	0.92	0.92	0.92	763
weighted avg	0.92	0.92	0.92	763

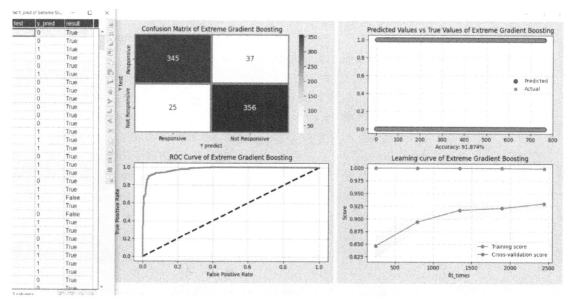

Figure 36 The results of using Extreme Gradient Boosting

The output is the evaluation result of the Extreme Gradient Boosting (XGBoost) classifier. Let's break down the metrics and analyze the model's performance:

- Accuracy: The accuracy of the model is approximately 91.87%, which means that it correctly predicts the class labels for about 91.87% of the total samples in the test dataset.

- Recall (Sensitivity): The recall is approximately 91.87% for both classes. This metric measures the model's ability to correctly identify positive samples (class 1) and negative samples (class 0). A high recall indicates that the model effectively captures true positive cases while minimizing false negatives.

- Precision: The precision of the model is approximately 91.92% for class 0 and 91.91% for class 1. Precision measures how many of the predicted positive cases are actually true positives. A high precision suggests that when the model predicts a positive class, it is correct most of the time.

- F1-Score: The F1-score is approximately 91.87% for both classes. The F1-score is the harmonic mean of precision and recall and provides a balanced measure of a model's performance. It considers both false positives and false negatives and is particularly useful when dealing with imbalanced datasets.

- Classification Report: The classification report provides a summary of precision, recall, and F1-score for each class (0 and 1). It also includes support, which represents the number of samples for each class.

In conclusion, the Extreme Gradient Boosting (XGBoost) classifier performs well on the given dataset, achieving high accuracy, recall, precision, and F1-scores for both classes. These metrics indicate that the model effectively discriminates between the two classes and makes accurate predictions. The balanced F1-scores suggest that the model is suitable for tasks where both precision and recall are essential, such as binary classification problems with imbalanced classes.

Multi-Layer Perceptron Classifier and Grid Search

In Machine_Learning class, define a new method named multi_layer_perceptron() as follows:

```python
def multi_layer_perceptron(self, name, X_train, X_test, y_train, y_test):
    # Define the parameter grid for the grid search
    param_grid = {
        'hidden_layer_sizes': [(50,), (100,), (50, 50), (100, 50), (100, 100)],
        'activation': ['logistic', 'relu'],
        'solver': ['adam', 'sgd'],
        'alpha': [0.0001, 0.001, 0.01],
        'learning_rate': ['constant', 'invscaling', 'adaptive'],
    }

    # Initialize the MLP Classifier
    mlp = MLPClassifier(random_state=2021)

    # Create GridSearchCV with the MLP Classifier and the parameter grid
    grid_search = GridSearchCV(mlp, param_grid, cv=3, scoring='accuracy', n_jobs=-1)

    # Train and perform grid search
    grid_search.fit(X_train, y_train)

    # Get the best MLP Classifier model from the grid search
    best_model = grid_search.best_estimator_

    #Saves model
    joblib.dump(best_model, 'MLP_Model.pkl')

    # Print the best hyperparameters found
    print(f"Best Hyperparameters for MLP:")
    print(grid_search.best_params_)

    return best_model
```

The multi_layer_perceptron() function is a part of a machine learning pipeline for training and evaluating a Multi-Layer Perceptron (MLP) classifier. Let's break down the key components of this function:

1. Parameter Grid: You've defined a parameter grid param_grid that includes various hyperparameters for tuning the MLP model. These hyperparameters include the architecture of the neural network (hidden layer sizes), activation functions, optimization algorithms, regularization strength (alpha), and learning rate scheduling.

2. MLP Classifier Initialization: You initialize an instance of the MLP Classifier with a fixed random seed (random_state=2021). The MLP Classifier is a type of artificial neural network used for classification tasks.

3. Grid Search: You create a GridSearchCV object named grid_search, which will perform an exhaustive search over the hyperparameter grid defined earlier. Grid search is used to find the best combination of hyperparameters for the MLP model.

4. Training and Grid Search: You fit (train) the MLP model on the training data (X_train, y_train) using the GridSearchCV object. This trains multiple MLP models with different hyperparameter combinations and evaluates their performance using cross-validation (cv=3).

5. Best Model Selection: After the grid search is complete, you obtain the best MLP model from the grid search results using grid_search.best_estimator_.

6. Model Saving: If desired, you save the best MLP model to a file named 'MLP_Model.pkl' using joblib. This allows you to reuse the trained model without having to retrain it in the future.

7. Printing Best Hyperparameters: You print out the best hyperparameters found by the grid search. This information helps you understand which hyperparameters contributed to the best model's performance.

Overall, this function automates the process of hyperparameter tuning for an MLP classifier and allows you to efficiently search for the best configuration to achieve optimal performance on the classification task.

Then, in Machine_Learning class, define a new method named implement_MLP():

```
def implement_MLP(self, chosen, X_train, X_test, y_train, y_test):
    file_path = os.getcwd()+"/MLP_Model.pkl"
    if os.path.exists(file_path):
        model = joblib.load('MLP_Model.pkl')
        y_pred = self.run_model(chosen, model, X_train, X_test, y_train, y_test, proba=True)
    else:
        model = self.multi_layer_perceptron(chosen, X_train, X_test, y_train, y_test)
        y_pred = self.run_model(chosen, model, X_train, X_test, y_train, y_test, proba=True)

    #Saves result into excel file
    self.obj_data.save_result(y_test, y_pred, "results_MLP.csv")

    print("Training Multi-Layer Perceptron done...")
    return model, y_pred
```

The implement_MLP() function is part of a machine learning pipeline and is used to implement and evaluate a Multi-Layer Perceptron (MLP) classifier for a given dataset. Let's break down the key components of this function:

1. Model Loading or Training: First, the function checks if a pre-trained MLP model exists in a file named 'MLP_Model.pkl' in the current working directory. If the file exists, it loads the pre-trained model using joblib.load. If not, it proceeds to train a new MLP model.

2. Model Training: If a pre-trained model does not exist, the function calls the multi_layer_perceptron() function, passing the chosen configuration, training data (X_train and y_train), and testing data (X_test and y_test). This function performs hyperparameter tuning and training of the MLP model.

3. Model Evaluation: After either loading the pre-trained model or training a new one, the function uses the trained model to make predictions on the testing data (X_test) by calling the run_model function. It requests probabilistic predictions (proba=True), indicating that it wants probability scores for each class.

4. Result Saving: The actual and predicted values (probabilities) are saved into an Excel file named 'results_MLP.csv' using the save_result() method of the obj_data object. This allows for later analysis and comparison of the model's performance.

5. Print Status: Finally, the function prints a message indicating that the training or loading of the MLP model is complete.

Overall, this function handles the entire pipeline of training and evaluating an MLP classifier, including the option to load a pre-trained model if one exists. This approach saves time and resources by avoiding unnecessary retraining of models when the same configuration has been trained previously.

Then, in Helper_Plot class, add this code to the end of choose_plot_ML() method:

```
if chosen == "Multi-Layer Perceptron":
    best_model, y_pred = self.obj_ml.implement_MLP(chosen, X_train, X_test, y_train, y_test)

    #Plots confusion matrix and ROC
    self.plot_cm_roc(best_model, X_test, y_test, y_pred, chosen, figure1, canvas1)

    #Plots true values versus predicted values diagram and learning curve
    self.plot_real_pred_val_learning_curve(best_model, X_train, y_train,
        X_test, y_test, y_pred, chosen, figure2, canvas2)

    #Shows table of result
    df_lr = self.obj_data.read_dataset("results_MLP.csv")
    self.shows_table(root, df_lr, 450, 750, "Y_test and Y_pred of Multi-Layer Perceptron")
```

Here's what it does step by step:

1. Model Implementation (implement_MLP()): If the chosen model is "Multi-Layer Perceptron," it loads a pre-trained MLP model if it exists (saved as a file named "MLP_Model.pkl" in the current working directory). If the pre-trained model doesn't

exist, it trains a new MLP model using grid search to find the best hyperparameters. Then, it uses this model to make predictions on the test data.

2. Performance Visualization (plot_cm_roc() and plot_real_pred_val_learning_curve()): After obtaining the predictions from the MLP model, it proceeds to create two types of plots:

   - Confusion Matrix and ROC Curve (plot_cm_roc()): It generates a confusion matrix and ROC curve to visually evaluate the performance of the MLP model on the test data.

   - True Values versus Predicted Values Diagram and Learning Curve (plot_real_pred_val_learning_curve): It creates a diagram that compares the true values to the predicted values. Additionally, it plots a learning curve to illustrate how the model's performance changes with different training dataset sizes.

3. Results Presentation (shows_table): It loads the results of the MLP model from an Excel file named "results_MLP.csv." This Excel file contains various performance metrics for the model. It then displays these results in a table within the GUI.

In summary, this section of the code focuses on training, evaluating, and visualizing the performance of an MLP classifier. It includes features like loading pre-trained models, conducting hyperparameter tuning with grid search, and presenting the results through various visualizations and tables.

Run main_class.py. Next, click on SPLIT DATA button. Then, choose Multi-Layer Perceptron to see the result of using Multi-Layer Perceptron classifier as shown in figure 37.

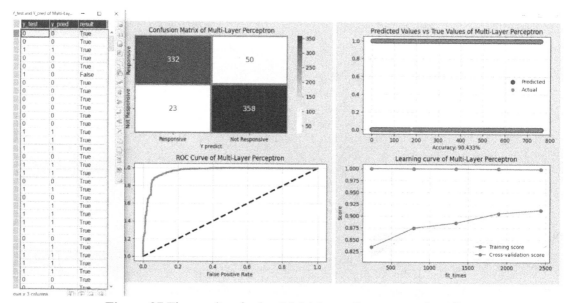

Figure 37 The results of using Multi-Layer Perceptron classifier

Output:
Multi-Layer Perceptron
accuracy: 0.9043250327653998
recall: 0.9043250327653998
precision: 0.9063689747768858
f1: 0.9042095303827421

	precision	recall	f1-score	support
0	0.94	0.87	0.90	382
1	0.88	0.94	0.91	381
accuracy			0.90	763
macro avg	0.91	0.90	0.90	763
weighted avg	0.91	0.90	0.90	763

The output is the performance evaluation of the Multi-Layer Perceptron (MLP) classifier. Let's break down the key metrics and their implications:

- Accuracy: Accuracy measures the overall correctness of the model's predictions. In this case, the MLP classifier achieved an accuracy of approximately 90.43%. This means that about 90.43% of the test data samples were classified correctly by the model.

- Recall (Sensitivity): Recall quantifies the model's ability to correctly identify positive instances out of all actual positive instances. For the positive class (class 1), the MLP classifier achieved a recall of approximately 90.43%. This indicates that the model correctly identified around 90.43% of all actual positive cases.

- Precision: Precision gauges the model's precision in correctly predicting positive instances. The MLP classifier achieved a precision of approximately 90.64% for the positive class. This means that among all instances predicted as positive, around 90.64% were indeed positive.

- F1-Score: The F1-score is the harmonic mean of precision and recall, providing a balance between these two metrics. For the positive class, the MLP classifier achieved an F1-score of approximately 90.42%. A higher F1-score indicates a better balance between precision and recall.

- Classification Report: The classification report provides a summary of precision, recall, and F1-score for each class (0 and 1). It also shows the support, which is the number of actual occurrences of each class in the test dataset.

Here's a conclusion based on the performance metrics:
The Multi-Layer Perceptron (MLP) classifier performed reasonably well on the test dataset, with an accuracy of approximately 90.43%. It showed a balanced performance between precision and recall, with F1-scores close to 0.90 for both classes. This suggests that the MLP classifier is effective in correctly classifying instances from both classes (0 and 1). However, further domain-

specific analysis may be necessary to determine whether this level of performance meets the specific requirements of the problem at hand.

Support Vector Classifier and Grid Search

In Machine_Learning class, define a new method named support_vector() as follows:

```python
def support_vector(self, name, X_train, X_test, y_train, y_test):
    #Support Vector Classifier
    # Define the parameter grid for the grid search
    param_grid = {
        'C': [0.1, 1, 10],
        'kernel': ['linear', 'poly', 'rbf'],
        'gamma': ['scale', 'auto', 0.1, 1],
    }

    # Initialize the SVC model
    model_svc = SVC(random_state=2021, probability=True)

    # Create GridSearchCV with the SVC model and the parameter grid
    grid_search = GridSearchCV(model_svc, param_grid, cv=3, scoring='accuracy', n_jobs=-1, refit=True)

    # Train and perform grid search
    grid_search.fit(X_train, y_train)

    # Get the best MLP Classifier model from the grid search
    best_model = grid_search.best_estimator_

    #Saves model
    joblib.dump(best_model, 'SVC_Model.pkl')

    # Print the best hyperparameters found
    print(f"Best Hyperparameters for SVC:")
    print(grid_search.best_params_)

    return best_model
```

The support_vector() function is for training a Support Vector Classifier (SVC) and performing hyperparameter tuning using grid search. Here's an explanation of each part of the function:

1. Parameter Grid Definition: You define a parameter grid param_grid that includes the hyperparameters to be tuned during grid search. These hyperparameters are:
   - 'C': This parameter controls the regularization strength. You provide a list of potential values: [0.1, 1, 10].
   - 'kernel': The kernel function used for transforming the data. You specify three kernel options: 'linear', 'poly', and 'rbf'.
   - 'gamma': This parameter defines the kernel coefficient. You provide a list of values: ['scale', 'auto', 0.1, 1].

2. SVC Model Initialization: You initialize the Support Vector Classifier (SVC) model with specific settings. You set random_state=2021 for reproducibility and probability=True to enable probability estimates.

3. GridSearchCV Setup: You create a GridSearchCV object named grid_search. This object combines the SVC model with the parameter grid for hyperparameter tuning. It uses 3-fold cross-validation (cv=3), measures performance using accuracy (scoring='accuracy'), and utilizes all available CPU cores (n_jobs=-1).

4. Grid Search Training: You fit the grid_search object to the training data (X_train and y_train). This process performs an exhaustive search over the hyperparameter combinations specified in param_grid to find the best combination based on cross-validated accuracy.

5. Best Model Selection: After grid search is complete, you obtain the best SVC model (best_model) based on the hyperparameters that resulted in the highest cross-validated accuracy.

6. Model Saving: The best model is saved to a file named 'SVC_Model.pkl' using the joblib.dump() function.

7. Printing Hyperparameters: You print the best hyperparameters found during the grid search.

The function returns the best trained SVC model with the selected hyperparameters.

This code demonstrates the process of hyperparameter tuning for an SVC model using grid search, helping you find the best combination of hyperparameters that optimizes the model's performance on the training data.

Then, in Machine_Learning class, define a new method named implement_SVC():

```python
def implement_SVC(self, chosen, X_train, X_test, y_train, y_test):
    file_path = os.getcwd()+"/SVC_Model.pkl"
    if os.path.exists(file_path):
        model = joblib.load('SVC_Model.pkl')
        y_pred = self.run_model(chosen, model, X_train, X_test, y_train, y_test, proba=True)
    else:
        model = self.support_vector(chosen, X_train, X_test, y_train, y_test)
        y_pred = self.run_model(chosen, model, X_train, X_test, y_train, y_test, proba=True)

    #Saves result into excel file
    self.obj_data.save_result(y_test, y_pred, "results_SVC.csv")

    print("Training Support Vector Classifier done...")
    return model, y_pred
```

The implement_SVC() function is responsible for training a Support Vector Classifier (SVC) model and performing predictions. Here's a breakdown of the function:

1. File Path Checking: It first checks if a pre-trained SVC model exists in a file named 'SVC_Model.pkl' in the current working directory (os.getcwd()). If the file exists, it loads the pre-trained model using joblib.load. If not, it proceeds to train a new model.

2. Model Training or Loading: If a pre-trained model doesn't exist, it calls the support_vector() function to train a new SVC model. This function performs hyperparameter tuning and returns the best model. The newly trained or loaded model is stored in the model variable.

3. Model Prediction: The function uses the trained or loaded model (model) to make predictions on the input data (X_train, X_test, y_train, y_test) using the run_model() function with proba=True. This means it returns probability estimates.

4. Saving Predictions: The function saves the predicted values (y_pred) and the corresponding true values (y_test) into an Excel file named "results_SVC.csv" using the save_result function.

5. Print Status: It prints a message indicating that the training of the Support Vector Classifier is complete.

6. Return Values: The function returns two values: the trained or loaded SVC model (model) and the predicted values (y_pred).

This function essentially serves as a wrapper for training and using the SVC model, ensuring that if a pre-trained model exists, it's loaded, and if not, a new model is trained. It also handles the saving of prediction results for later analysis or reporting.

Then, in Helper_Plot class, add this code to the end of choose_plot_ML() method:

```
if chosen == "Support Vector Classifier":
    best_model, y_pred = self.obj_ml.implement_SVC(chosen, X_train, X_test, y_train, y_test)

    #Plots confusion matrix and ROC
    self.plot_cm_roc(best_model, X_test, y_test, y_pred, chosen, figure1, canvas1)

    #Plots true values versus predicted values diagram and learning curve
    self.plot_real_pred_val_learning_curve(best_model, X_train, y_train,
        X_test, y_test, y_pred, chosen, figure2, canvas2)

    #Shows table of result
    df_lr = self.obj_data.read_dataset("results_SVC.csv")
    self.shows_table(root, df_lr, 450, 750, "Y_test and Y_pred of Support Vector Classifier")
```

The code is for training and evaluating support vector classifier. Here's a summary of what this block of code does:

1. Model Selection: It checks if the selected machine learning model is a "Support Vector Classifier" (chosen == "Support Vector Classifier"). If the selected model matches, it proceeds to train and evaluate the Support Vector Classifier. This is part of a graphical user interface (GUI) or command-line interface (CLI) where users can choose which machine learning model to train and evaluate.

2. Model Training: If the chosen model is a Support Vector Classifier, it calls the implement_SVC method to train the Support Vector Classifier using the provided training data (X_train, y_train) and make predictions on the test data (X_test). The trained model (best_model) and the predictions (y_pred) are returned.

3. Evaluation and Visualization: It then proceeds to evaluate the model and create visualizations:

   • It plots the confusion matrix and Receiver Operating Characteristic (ROC) curve for the Support Vector Classifier using the plot_cm_roc() method. These visualizations help assess the model's performance and its ability to distinguish between different classes.

   • It plots a diagram that compares true values versus predicted values and a learning curve using the plot_real_pred_val_learning_curve() method. This helps in visualizing how well the model's predictions align with the actual values and how its performance changes with different amounts of training data.

   • It displays a table of results obtained from the Support Vector Classifier using the shows_table() method. This table contains various evaluation metrics such as accuracy, precision, recall, and F1-score, comparing the model's predictions to the actual test data.

4. Result Storage: The code appears to store the evaluation results, possibly in an Excel file with the filename "results_SVC.csv" using the save_result() method. This allows for later analysis and comparison of results.

Overall, this code segment is a part of a larger machine learning pipeline designed for training, evaluating, and visualizing different machine learning models, with a focus on the Support Vector Classifier in this specific case. Users can select the model they want to work with, and the system handles the training, evaluation, and visualization of that model.

Run main_class.py. Next, click on SPLIT DATA button. Then, choose Suppport Vector Classifier to see the result of using Suppport Vector classifier as shown in figure 38.

Output:
Support Vector Classifier

```
accuracy:  0.9003931847968545
recall:  0.9003931847968545
precision:  0.9022701737370328
f1:  0.9002818528428114
```

	precision	recall	f1-score	support
0	0.93	0.87	0.90	382
1	0.87	0.93	0.90	381
accuracy			0.90	763
macro avg	0.90	0.90	0.90	763
weighted avg	0.90	0.90	0.90	763

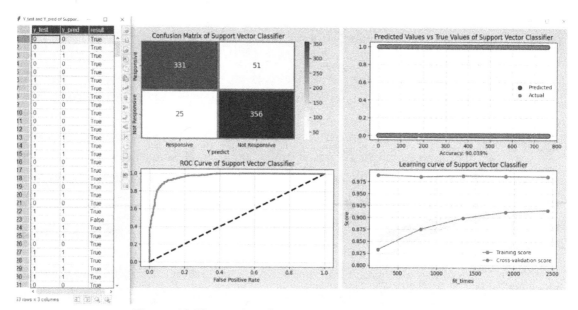

Figure 38 The results of using Support Vector classifier

The output is the evaluation result for the Support Vector Classifier (SVC) model. Here's a detailed analysis of the metrics and a conclusion based on the output:

- Model Name: Support Vector Classifier
- Overall Accuracy: 0.9004

  Accuracy represents the ratio of correctly predicted instances to the total number of instances in the dataset. In this case, the model achieves an accuracy of approximately 90.04%, indicating that it correctly classifies about 90.04% of the samples.

- Recall (Sensitivity): 0.9004

  Recall (also known as Sensitivity) measures the model's ability to correctly identify positive instances (in this case, class 1). A recall score of approximately 90.04% means that the model correctly identifies about 90.04% of all actual positive cases.

- Precision: 0.9023

  Precision represents the ratio of correctly predicted positive instances to all instances predicted as positive by the model. With a precision score of approximately 90.23%, the model correctly predicts about 90.23% of the instances it labels as positive.

- F1-Score: 0.9003

  The F1-score is the harmonic mean of precision and recall. It provides a balance between precision and recall. The F1-score of approximately 90.03% suggests that the model achieves a good balance between precision and recall.

- Classification Report:

  The classification report provides a breakdown of precision, recall, and F1-score for each class (0 and 1) individually.

  - For class 0 (usually the negative class), the precision is 0.93, recall is 0.87, and F1-score is 0.90.
  - For class 1 (usually the positive class), the precision is 0.87, recall is 0.93, and F1-score is 0.90.

  These values give insights into how well the model performs for each class separately.

Conclusion:

The Support Vector Classifier (SVC) model performs well on the given dataset with an overall accuracy of around 90.04%. It demonstrates a good balance between precision and recall, as indicated by the F1-score of approximately 90.03%. The model shows relatively consistent performance for both class 0 and class 1, with similar precision, recall, and F1-score values for both classes.

AdaBoost Classifier and Grid Search

In Machine_Learning class, define a new method named adaboost_classifier() as follows:

```python
def adaboost_classifier(self, name, X_train, X_test, y_train, y_test):
    # Define the parameter grid for the grid search
    param_grid = {
        'n_estimators': [50, 100, 150],
        'learning_rate': [0.01, 0.1, 0.2],
    }

    # Initialize the AdaBoost classifier
    adaboost = AdaBoostClassifier(random_state=2021)

    # Create GridSearchCV with the AdaBoost classifier and the parameter grid
    grid_search = GridSearchCV(adaboost, param_grid, cv=3, scoring='accuracy', n_jobs=-1)


    # Train and perform grid search
```

```
grid_search.fit(X_train, y_train)

# Get the best AdaBoost Classifier model from the grid search
best_model = grid_search.best_estimator_

#Saves model
joblib.dump(best_model, 'ADA_Model.pkl')

# Print the best hyperparameters found
print(f"Best Hyperparameters for AdaBoost:")
print(grid_search.best_params_)

return best_model
```

The code defines a function adaboost_classifier() that sets up an AdaBoost Classifier model and performs hyperparameter tuning using grid search. Here's an explanation of each part of the code:

1. Parameter Grid Definition:

    • param_grid is a dictionary that defines the hyperparameters to be tuned and the range of values to consider during the grid search.

    • It includes two hyperparameters:

        • n_estimators: The number of weak learners (base estimators) to train in the ensemble.

        • learning_rate: The contribution of each weak learner to the final prediction.

2. AdaBoost Classifier Initialization:

    An AdaBoost Classifier is initialized with random_state=2021. This classifier is an ensemble learning method that combines multiple weak learners to create a strong classifier.

3. Grid Search Setup:

    GridSearchCV is used to set up the grid search. It takes the AdaBoost classifier, the parameter grid (param_grid), and other configurations:

    • cv=3: Performs a 3-fold cross-validation during the grid search.

    • scoring='accuracy': Uses accuracy as the scoring metric to evaluate model performance.

    • n_jobs=-1: Utilizes all available CPU cores for parallel processing.

4. Grid Search Training:

    • The grid_search object is trained on the provided training data (X_train and y_train).

    • It performs an exhaustive search over the hyperparameter grid, fitting the AdaBoost Classifier with different hyperparameter combinations and evaluating their performance using cross-validation.

5. Best Model Selection:

After the grid search, the best-performing AdaBoost Classifier model is selected based on the hyperparameter combinations that resulted in the highest accuracy during cross-validation.

6. Model Saving:

The best model is saved using joblib.dump to a file named 'ADA_Model.pkl' for future use.

7. Print Hyperparameters:

The function prints the best hyperparameters found during the grid search.

The purpose of this function is to automate the process of hyperparameter tuning for an AdaBoost Classifier. It helps you find the optimal combination of hyperparameters that maximize the model's accuracy on the training data. The best model can then be used for making predictions on new data.

Then, in Machine_Learning class, define a new method named implement_ADA():

```
def implement_ADA(self, chosen, X_train, X_test, y_train, y_test):
    file_path = os.getcwd()+"/ADA_Model.pkl"
    if os.path.exists(file_path):
        model = joblib.load('ADA_Model.pkl')
        y_pred = self.run_model(chosen, model, X_train, X_test, y_train, y_test, proba=True)
    else:
        model = self.adaboost_classifier(chosen, X_train, X_test, y_train, y_test)
        y_pred = self.run_model(chosen, model, X_train, X_test, y_train, y_test, proba=True)

    #Saves result into excel file
    self.obj_data.save_result(y_test, y_pred, "results_ADA.csv")

    print("Training AdaBoost done...")
    return model, y_pred
```

The code defines a function implement_ADA() that implements an AdaBoost Classifier for a binary classification problem. Here's a breakdown of what the code does:

1. Model Loading or Training:
   - The function first checks if a saved AdaBoost Classifier model exists in a file named 'ADA_Model.pkl' in the current working directory.
   - If the model file exists, it loads the model using joblib.load. This is done to avoid retraining the model if it has already been trained and saved.
   - If the model file doesn't exist, it calls the adaboost_classifier() function to train a new AdaBoost Classifier. This function performs hyperparameter tuning using grid search and returns the best-trained model.

2. Model Prediction:

Regardless of whether the model was loaded or trained, the function uses the obtained AdaBoost Classifier model to make predictions on the provided test data (X_test).

3. Result Saving:

The predicted labels (y_pred) are saved along with the true labels (y_test) into an Excel file named "results_ADA.csv" using the save_result method of the obj_data object. This file contains metrics and results for model evaluation.

4. Printing Progress:

The function prints "Training AdaBoost done..." to indicate that the model has been either loaded or trained and predictions have been made.

5. Model and Predictions Return:

The function returns both the AdaBoost Classifier model and the predicted labels (y_pred) for further analysis or use.

This function essentially encapsulates the process of loading a pre-trained AdaBoost model (if available) or training a new one, making predictions on test data, and saving the results. It provides flexibility for reusing a trained model and avoids redundant training when the model has already been trained and saved in a previous run.

Then, in Helper_Plot class, add this code to the end of choose_plot_ML() method:

```
if chosen == "AdaBoost":
    best_model, y_pred = self.obj_ml.implement_ADA(chosen, X_train, X_test, y_train, y_test)

    #Plots confusion matrix and ROC
    self.plot_cm_roc(best_model, X_test, y_test, y_pred, chosen, figure1, canvas1)

    #Plots true values versus predicted values diagram and learning curve
    self.plot_real_pred_val_learning_curve(best_model, X_train, y_train,
        X_test, y_test, y_pred, chosen, figure2, canvas2)

    #Shows table of result
    df_lr = self.obj_data.read_dataset("results_ADA.csv")
    self.shows_table(root, df_lr, 450, 750, "Y_test and Y_pred of AdaBoost Classifier")
```

In this code, the program checks if the chosen machine learning algorithm is "AdaBoost." If it is indeed AdaBoost, the code proceeds with the following steps. First, it either loads a pre-trained AdaBoost Classifier model from a file or trains a new one if the model file doesn't exist. This trained model is used to make predictions on the test dataset, and the resulting predictions (y_pred) are stored. Next, the code generates various visualizations and reports for model evaluation. It creates a confusion matrix and ROC curve, illustrating the model's classification performance. Additionally, it plots a diagram comparing true values versus predicted values and a learning curve to analyze the model's behavior and performance over time.

Furthermore, the code reads the results from a previously saved Excel file named "results_ADA.csv," containing crucial metrics and statistics related to the AdaBoost Classifier's performance. It then displays these results in a tabular format within the graphical user interface (GUI), enhancing the user's ability to interpret and analyze the classifier's effectiveness. Overall, this code section streamlines the implementation, evaluation, and visualization of the AdaBoost Classifier, providing valuable insights into its performance for informed decision-making.

Run main_class.py. Next, click on SPLIT DATA button. Then, choose AdaBoost to see the result of using AdaBoost classifier as shown in figure 39.

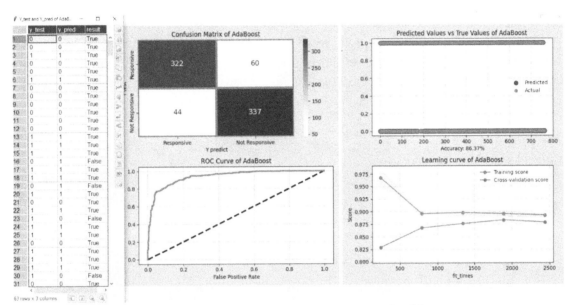

Figure 39 The results of using AdaBoost classifier

Output:
AdaBoost
accuracy: 0.8636959370904325
recall: 0.8636959370904325
precision: 0.8643442185483509
f1: 0.8636397238206017

	precision	recall	f1-score	support
0	0.88	0.84	0.86	382
1	0.85	0.88	0.87	381
accuracy			0.86	763
macro avg	0.86	0.86	0.86	763
weighted avg	0.86	0.86	0.86	763

The AdaBoost Classifier, as indicated by the output, achieved an accuracy of approximately 86.37% on the test dataset. This means that it correctly classified around 86.37% of the instances in the test set. The recall for both classes (0 and 1) is reasonably balanced, with a slightly higher recall for class 1 (positive class) compared to class 0 (negative class). Specifically, it achieved a recall of approximately 88% for class 1, implying that it correctly identified about 88% of the positive instances. For class 0, it had a recall of roughly 84%, indicating that it successfully recognized around 84% of the negative instances.

In terms of precision, the AdaBoost Classifier achieved good results, with precision values of approximately 88% for class 0 and 85% for class 1. This means that when the model predicted a certain class, it was correct about 88% of the time for class 0 and 85% of the time for class 1. The F1-score, which combines precision and recall into a single metric, is around 86.36% for class 0 and 87% for class 1. These F1-scores reflect the balance between precision and recall for each class. Overall, the AdaBoost Classifier demonstrated reasonable performance on this dataset, with good accuracy and balanced precision and recall values for both classes.

Following is the full source code:

```
#main_class.py
import tkinter as tk
from tkinter import *
from design_window import Design_Window
from process_data import Process_Data
from helper_plot import Helper_Plot
from machine_learning import Machine_Learning
import os

class Main_Class:
    def __init__(self, root):
        self.initialize()

    def initialize(self):
        self.root = root
        width = 1500
        height = 750
        self.root.geometry(f"{width}x{height}")
        self.root.title("TKINTER AND DATA SCIENCE")

        #Creates necessary objects
        self.obj_window = Design_Window()
        self.obj_data = Process_Data()
        self.obj_plot = Helper_Plot()
        self.obj_ML = Machine_Learning()

        #Reads dataset
        self.df = self.obj_data.preprocess()

        #Categorize dataset
        self.df_dummy = self.obj_data.categorize(self.df)
```

```
        #Extracts input and output variables
        self.cat_cols, self.num_cols = self.obj_data.extract_cat_num_cols(self.df)
        self.df_final = self.obj_data.encode_categorical_feats(self.df, self.cat_cols)
        self.X, self.y = self.obj_data.extract_input_output_vars(self.df_final)

        #Places widgets in root
        self.obj_window.add_widgets(self.root)

        #Binds event
        self.binds_event()

        #Initially turns off combo4 and combo5 before data splitting is done
        self.obj_window.combo4['state'] = 'disabled'
        self.obj_window.combo5['state'] = 'disabled'

    def binds_event(self):
        #Binds listbox to a function
        self.obj_window.listbox.bind("<<ListboxSelect>>", self.choose_list_widget)

        # Binds combobox1 to a function
        self.obj_window.combo1.bind("<<ComboboxSelected>>", self.choose_combobox1)

        # Binds combobox2 to a function
        self.obj_window.combo2.bind("<<ComboboxSelected>>", self.choose_combobox2)

        #Binds button1 to shows_table() function
        #Shows table if user clicks LOAD DATASET
        self.obj_window.button1.config(command = lambda:self.obj_plot.shows_table(self.root, self.df, 1400, 600,
"Dataset"))
        #Binds button2 to train_ML() function
        self.obj_window.button2.config(command=self.train_ML)

        # Binds combobox4 to a function
        self.obj_window.combo4.bind("<<ComboboxSelected>>", self.choose_combobox4)

    def choose_list_widget(self, event):
        chosen = self.obj_window.listbox.get(self.obj_window.listbox.curselection())
        print(chosen)
        self.obj_plot.choose_plot(self.df, self.df_dummy, chosen,
            self.obj_window.figure1, self.obj_window.canvas1,
            self.obj_window.figure2, self.obj_window.canvas2)

    def choose_combobox1(self, event):
        chosen = self.obj_window.combo1.get()
        self.obj_plot.choose_category(self.df_dummy, chosen,
            self.obj_window.figure1, self.obj_window.canvas1,
            self.obj_window.figure2, self.obj_window.canvas2)

    def choose_combobox2(self, event):
        chosen = self.obj_window.combo2.get()
        self.obj_plot.choose_plot_more(self.df_final, chosen,
            self.X, self.y,
            self.obj_window.figure1,
            self.obj_window.canvas1, self.obj_window.figure2,
            self.obj_window.canvas2)
```

```python
    def train_ML(self):
        file_path = os.getcwd()+"/X_train.pkl"
        if os.path.exists(file_path):
            self.X_train, self.X_test, self.y_train, self.y_test = self.obj_ML.load_files()
        else:
            self.obj_ML.oversampling_splitting(self.X, self.y)
            self.X_train, self.X_test, self.y_train, self.y_test = self.obj_ML.load_files()

        print("Loading files done...")

        #turns on combo4 and combo5 after splitting is done
        self.obj_window.combo4['state'] = 'normal'
        self.obj_window.combo5['state'] = 'normal'

        self.obj_window.button2.config(state="disabled")

    def choose_combobox4(self, event):
        chosen = self.obj_window.combo4.get()
        self.obj_plot.choose_plot_ML(self.root, chosen, self.X_train, self.X_test,
            self.y_train, self.y_test, self.obj_window.figure1,
            self.obj_window.canvas1, self.obj_window.figure2,
            self.obj_window.canvas2)

if __name__ == "__main__":
    root = tk.Tk()
    app = Main_Class(root)
    root.mainloop()


#design_window.py
import tkinter as tk
from tkinter import ttk
from matplotlib.figure import Figure
from matplotlib.backends.backend_tkagg import FigureCanvasTkAgg

class Design_Window:
    def add_widgets(self, root):
        #Adds button(s)
        self.add_buttons(root)

        #Adds canvasses
        self.add_canvas(root)

        #Adds labels
        self.add_labels(root)

        #Adds listbox widget
        self.add_listboxes(root)

        #Adds combobox widget
        self.add_comboboxes(root)

    def add_buttons(self, root):
        #Adds button
        self.button1 = tk.Button(root, height=2, width=30, text="LOAD DATASET")
        self.button1.grid(row=0, column=0, padx=5, pady=5, sticky="w")
```

```python
        self.button2 = tk.Button(root, height=2, width=30, text="SPLIT DATA")
        self.button2.grid(row=9, column=0, padx=5, pady=5, sticky="w")

    def add_labels(self, root):
        #Adds labels
        self.label1 = tk.Label(root, text = "CHOOSE PLOT", fg = "red")
        self.label1.grid(row=1, column=0, padx=5, pady=1, sticky="w")

        self.label2 = tk.Label(root, text = "CHOOSE CATEGORIZED PLOT", fg = "blue")
        self.label2.grid(row=3, column=0, padx=5, pady=1, sticky="w")

        self.label2 = tk.Label(root, text = "CHOOSE FEATURES", fg = "black")
        self.label2.grid(row=5, column=0, padx=5, pady=1, sticky="w")

        self.label3 = tk.Label(root, text = "CHOOSE REGRESSORS", fg = "green")
        self.label3.grid(row=7, column=0, padx=5, pady=1, sticky="w")

        self.label4 = tk.Label(root, text = "CHOOSE MACHINE LEARNING", fg = "blue")
        self.label4.grid(row=10, column=0, padx=5, pady=1, sticky="w")

        self.label5 = tk.Label(root, text = "CHOOSE DEEP LEARNING", fg = "red")
        self.label5.grid(row=12, column=0, padx=5, pady=1, sticky="w")

    def add_canvas(self, root):
        #Menambahkan canvas1 widget pada root untuk menampilkan hasil
        self.figure1 = Figure(figsize=(6.2, 7), dpi=100)
        self.figure1.patch.set_facecolor("lightgray")
        self.canvas1 = FigureCanvasTkAgg(self.figure1, master=root)
        self.canvas1.get_tk_widget().grid(row=0, column=1, columnspan=1, rowspan=25, padx=5, pady=5, sticky="n")

        #Menambahkan canvas2 widget pada root untuk menampilkan hasil
        self.figure2 = Figure(figsize=(6.2, 7), dpi=100)
        self.figure2.patch.set_facecolor("lightgray")
        self.canvas2 = FigureCanvasTkAgg(self.figure2, master=root)
        self.canvas2.get_tk_widget().grid(row=0, column=2, columnspan=1, rowspan=25, padx=5, pady=5, sticky="n")

    def add_listboxes(self, root):
        #Menambahkan list widget
        self.listbox = tk.Listbox(root, selectmode=tk.SINGLE, width=35)
        self.listbox.grid(row=2, column=0, sticky='n', padx=5, pady=1)

        # Menyisipkan item ke dalam list widget
        items = ["Marital Status", "Education", "Country",
            "Age Group", "Education with Response 0", "Education with Response 1",
            "Country with Response 0", "Country with Response 1",
            "Customer Age", "Income", "Mount of Wines",
            "Education versus Response", "Age Group versus Response",
            "Marital Status versus Response", "Country versus Response",
            "Number of Dependants versus Response",
            "Country versus Customer Age Per Education",
            "Num_TotalPurchases versus Education Per Marital Status"]
        for item in items:
            self.listbox.insert(tk.END, item)

        self.listbox.config(height=len(items))
```

```python
    def add_comboboxes(self, root):
        # Create ComboBoxes
        self.combo1 = ttk.Combobox(root, width=32)
        self.combo1["values"] = ["Categorized Income versus Response",
            "Categorized Total Purchase versus Categorized Income",
            "Categorized Recency versus Categorized Total Purchase",
            "Categorized Customer Month versus Categorized Customer Age",
            "Categorized Mount of Gold Products versus Categorized Income",
            "Categorized Mount of Fish Products versus Categorized Total AmountSpent",
            "Categorized Mount of Meat Products versus Categorized Recency",
            "Distribution of Numerical Columns"]
        self.combo1.grid(row=4, column=0, padx=5, pady=1, sticky="n")

        self.combo2 = ttk.Combobox(root, width=32)
        self.combo2["values"] = ["Correlation Matrix", "RF Features Importance",
            "ET Features Importance", "RFE Features Importance"]
        self.combo2.grid(row=6, column=0, padx=5, pady=1, sticky="n")

        self.combo3 = ttk.Combobox(root, width=32)
        self.combo3["values"] = ["Linear Regression", "RF Regression",
            "Decision Trees Regression", "KNN Regression",
            "AdaBoost Regression", "Gradient Boosting Regression",
            "XGB Regression", "LGB Regression", "CatBoost Regression",
            "SVR Regression", "Lasso Regression", "Ridge Regression"]
        self.combo3.grid(row=8, column=0, padx=5, pady=1, sticky="n")

        self.combo4 = ttk.Combobox(root, width=32)
        self.combo4["values"] = ["Logistic Regression", "Random Forest",
            "Decision Trees", "K-Nearest Neighbors",
            "AdaBoost", "Gradient Boosting",
            "Extreme Gradient Boosting", "Light Gradient Boosting",
            "Multi-Layer Perceptron", "Support Vector Classifier"]
        self.combo4.grid(row=11, column=0, padx=5, pady=1, sticky="n")

        self.combo5 = ttk.Combobox(root, width=32)
        self.combo5["values"] = ["LSTM", "Convolutional NN", "Recurrent NN", "Feed-Forward NN", "Artifical NN"]
        self.combo5.grid(row=13, column=0, padx=5, pady=1, sticky="n")

#helper_plot.py
from tkinter import *
import seaborn as sns
import numpy as np
from pandastable import Table
from process_data import Process_Data
from machine_learning import Machine_Learning
from sklearn.metrics import confusion_matrix, roc_curve, accuracy_score
from sklearn.model_selection import learning_curve

class Helper_Plot:
    def __init__(self):
        self.obj_data = Process_Data()
        self.obj_ml = Machine_Learning()
        # self.obj_dl = Deep_Learning()

    def shows_table(self, root, df, width, height, title):
```

```
      frame = Toplevel(root) #new window
      self.table = Table(frame, dataframe=df, showtoolbar=True, showstatusbar=True)

      # Sets dimension of Toplevel
      frame.geometry(f"{width}x{height}")
      frame.title(title)
      self.table.show()

  # Defines function to create pie chart and bar plot as subplots
  def plot_piechart(self, df, var, figure, canvas, title="):
      figure.clear()

      # Pie Chart (Subplot kiri)
      plot1 = figure.add_subplot(2,1,1)
      label_list = list(df[var].value_counts().index)
      colors = sns.color_palette("deep", len(label_list))
      _, _, autopcts = plot1.pie(df[var].value_counts(), autopct="%1.1f%%", colors=colors,
          startangle=30, labels=label_list,
          wedgeprops={"linewidth": 2, "edgecolor": "white"},  # Add white edge
          shadow=True, textprops={'fontsize': 7})
      plot1.set_title("Distribution of " + var + " variable " + title, fontsize=10)

      # Bar Plot (Subplot Kanan)
      plot2 = figure.add_subplot(2,1,2)
      ax = df[var].value_counts().plot(kind="barh", color=colors, alpha=0.8, ax = plot2)
      for i, j in enumerate(df[var].value_counts().values):
          ax.text(.7, i, j, weight="bold", fontsize=7)

      plot2.set_title("Count of " + var + " cases " + title, fontsize=10)

      figure.tight_layout()
      canvas.draw()

  def another_versus_response(self, df, feat, num_bins, figure, canvas):
      figure.clear()
      plot1 = figure.add_subplot(2,1,1)

      colors = sns.color_palette("Set2")
      df[df['Response'] == 0][feat].plot(ax=plot1, kind='hist', bins=num_bins, edgecolor='black', color=colors[0])
      plot1.set_title('Not Responsive', fontsize=15)
      plot1.set_xlabel(feat, fontsize=10)
      plot1.set_ylabel('Count', fontsize=10)
      data1 = []
      for p in plot1.patches:
          x = p.get_x() + p.get_width() / 2.
          y = p.get_height()
          plot1.annotate(format(y, '.0f'), (x, y), ha='center',
              va='center', xytext=(0, 10),
              weight="bold", fontsize=7, textcoords='offset points')
          data1.append([x, y])

      plot2 = figure.add_subplot(2,1,2)
      df[df['Response'] == 1][feat].plot(ax=plot2, kind='hist', bins=num_bins, edgecolor='black', color=colors[1])
      plot2.set_title('Responsive', fontsize=15)
      plot2.set_xlabel(feat, fontsize=10)
      plot2.set_ylabel('Count', fontsize=10)
```

```python
        data2 = []
        for p in plot2.patches:
            x = p.get_x() + p.get_width() / 2.
            y = p.get_height()
            plot1.annotate(format(y, '.0f'), (x, y), ha='center',
                va='center', xytext=(0, 10),
                weight="bold", fontsize=7, textcoords='offset points')
            data2.append([x, y])

        figure.tight_layout()
        canvas.draw()

    #Puts label inside stacked bar
    def put_label_stacked_bar(self, ax,fontsize):
        #patches is everything inside of the chart
        for rect in ax.patches:
            # Find where everything is located
            height = rect.get_height()
            width = rect.get_width()
            x = rect.get_x()
            y = rect.get_y()

            # The height of the bar is the data value and can be used as the label
            label_text = f'{height:.0f}'

            # ax.text(x, y, text)
            label_x = x + width / 2
            label_y = y + height / 2

            # plots only when height is greater than specified value
            if height > 0:
                ax.text(label_x, label_y, label_text, \
                    ha='center', va='center', \
                    weight = "bold",fontsize=fontsize)

    #Plots one variable against another variable
    def dist_one_vs_another_plot(self, df, cat1, cat2, figure, canvas, title):
        figure.clear()
        plot1 = figure.add_subplot(1,1,1)

        group_by_stat = df.groupby([cat1, cat2]).size()
        colors = sns.color_palette("Set2", len(df[cat1].unique()))
        stacked_data = group_by_stat.unstack()
        group_by_stat.unstack().plot(kind='bar', stacked=True, ax=plot1, grid=True, color=colors)
        plot1.set_title(title, fontsize=12)
        plot1.set_ylabel('Number of Cases', fontsize=10)
        plot1.set_xlabel(cat1, fontsize=10)
        self.put_label_stacked_bar(plot1,7)
        # Set font for tick labels
        plot1.tick_params(axis='both', which='major', labelsize=8)
        plot1.tick_params(axis='both', which='minor', labelsize=8)
        plot1.legend(fontsize=8)
        figure.tight_layout()
        canvas.draw()

    def box_plot(self, df, x, y, hue, figure, canvas, title):
```

```
    figure.clear()
    plot1 = figure.add_subplot(1,1,1)

    #Creates boxplot of Num_TotalPurchases versus Num_Dependants
    sns.boxplot(data = df, x = x, y = y, hue = hue, ax=plot1)
    plot1.set_title(title, fontsize=14)
    plot1.set_xlabel(x, fontsize=10)
    plot1.set_ylabel(y, fontsize=10)
    figure.tight_layout()
    canvas.draw()

def choose_plot(self, df1, df2, chosen, figure1, canvas1, figure2, canvas2):
    print(chosen)
    if chosen == "Marital Status":
        self.plot_piechart(df2, "Marital_Status", figure1, canvas1)

    elif chosen == "Education":
        self.plot_piechart(df2, "Education", figure2, canvas2)

    elif chosen == "Country":
        self.plot_piechart(df2, "Country", figure1, canvas1)

    elif chosen == "Age Group":
        self.plot_piechart(df2, "AgeGroup", figure2, canvas2)

    elif chosen == "Age Group":
        self.plot_piechart(df2, "AgeGroup", figure2, canvas2)

    elif chosen == "Education with Response 0":
        self.plot_piechart(df2[df2.Response==0], "Education", figure1, canvas1, " with Response 0")

    elif chosen == "Education with Response 1":
        self.plot_piechart(df2[df2.Response==1], "Education", figure2, canvas2, " with Response 1")

    elif chosen == "Country with Response 0":
        self.plot_piechart(df2[df2.Response==0], "Country", figure1, canvas1, " with Response 0")

    elif chosen == "Country with Response 1":
        self.plot_piechart(df2[df2.Response==1], "Country", figure2, canvas2, " with Response 1")

    elif chosen == "Income":
        self.another_versus_response(df1, "Income", 32, figure1, canvas1)

    elif chosen == "Mount of Wines":
        self.another_versus_response(df1, "MntWines", 32, figure2, canvas2)

    elif chosen == "Customer Age":
        self.another_versus_response(df1, "Customer_Age", 32, figure1, canvas1)

    elif chosen == "Education versus Response":
        self.dist_one_vs_another_plot(df2, "Education", "Response", figure2, canvas2, chosen)

    elif chosen == "Age Group versus Response":
        self.dist_one_vs_another_plot(df2, "AgeGroup", "Response", figure1, canvas1, chosen)

    elif chosen == "Marital Status versus Response":
```

```
        self.dist_one_vs_another_plot(df2, "Marital_Status", "Response", figure2, canvas2, chosen)

    elif chosen == "Country versus Response":
        self.dist_one_vs_another_plot(df2, "Country", "Response", figure1, canvas1, chosen)

    elif chosen == "Number of Dependants versus Response":
        self.dist_one_vs_another_plot(df2, "Num_Dependants", "Response", figure2, canvas2, chosen)

    elif chosen == "Country versus Customer Age Per Education":
        self.box_plot(df1, "Country", "Customer_Age", "Education", figure1, canvas1, chosen)

    elif chosen == "Num_TotalPurchases versus Education Per Marital Status":
        self.box_plot(df1, "Education", "Num_TotalPurchases", "Marital_Status", figure2, canvas2, chosen)

def choose_category(self, df, chosen, figure1, canvas1, figure2, canvas2):
    if chosen == "Categorized Income versus Response":
        self.dist_one_vs_another_plot(df, "Income", "Response", figure1, canvas1, chosen)

    if chosen == "Categorized Total Purchase versus Categorized Income":
        self.dist_one_vs_another_plot(df, "Num_TotalPurchases", "Income", figure2, canvas2, chosen)

    if chosen == "Categorized Recency versus Categorized Total Purchase":
        self.dist_one_vs_another_plot(df, "Recency", "Num_TotalPurchases", figure1, canvas1, chosen)

    if chosen == "Categorized Customer Month versus Categorized Customer Age":
        self.dist_one_vs_another_plot(df, "Dt_Customer_Month", "Customer_Age", figure2, canvas2, chosen)

    if chosen == "Categorized Mount of Gold Products versus Categorized Income":
        self.dist_one_vs_another_plot(df, "MntGoldProds", "Income", figure1, canvas1, chosen)

    if chosen == "Categorized Mount of Fish Products versus Categorized Total AmountSpent":
        self.dist_one_vs_another_plot(df, "MntFishProducts", "TotalAmount_Spent", figure2, canvas2, chosen)

    if chosen == "Categorized Mount of Meat Products versus Categorized Recency":
        self.dist_one_vs_another_plot(df, "MntMeatProducts", "Recency", figure1, canvas1, chosen)

def plot_corr_mat(self, df, figure, canvas):
    figure.clear()
    plot1 = figure.add_subplot(1,1,1)
    categorical_columns = df.select_dtypes(include=['object', 'category']).columns
    df_removed = df.drop(columns=categorical_columns)
    corrdata = df_removed.corr()

    annot_kws = {"size": 5}
    sns.heatmap(corrdata, ax = plot1, lw=1, annot=True, cmap="Reds", annot_kws=annot_kws)
    plot1.set_title('Correlation Matrix', fontweight ="bold",fontsize=14)

    # Set font for x and y labels
    plot1.set_xlabel('Features', fontweight="bold", fontsize=12)
    plot1.set_ylabel('Features', fontweight="bold", fontsize=12)

    # Set font for tick labels
    plot1.tick_params(axis='both', which='major', labelsize=5)
    plot1.tick_params(axis='both', which='minor', labelsize=5)

    figure.tight_layout()
```

```
    canvas.draw()

def plot_rf_importance(self, X, y, figure, canvas):
    result_rf = self.obj_data.feat_importance_rf(X, y)
    figure.clear()
    plot1 = figure.add_subplot(1,1,1)
    sns.set_color_codes("pastel")
    ax=sns.barplot(x = 'Values',y = 'Features', data=result_rf, color="Blue", ax=plot1)
    plot1.set_title('Random Forest Features Importance', fontweight ="bold",fontsize=14)

    plot1.set_xlabel('Features Importance',  fontsize=10)
    plot1.set_ylabel('Feature Labels',  fontsize=10)
    # Set font for tick labels
    plot1.tick_params(axis='both', which='major', labelsize=5)
    plot1.tick_params(axis='both', which='minor', labelsize=5)
    figure.tight_layout()
    canvas.draw()

def plot_et_importance(self, X, y, figure, canvas):
    result_rf = self.obj_data.feat_importance_et(X, y)
    figure.clear()
    plot1 = figure.add_subplot(1,1,1)
    sns.set_color_codes("pastel")
    ax=sns.barplot(x = 'Values',y = 'Features', data=result_rf, color="Red", ax=plot1)
    plot1.set_title('Extra Trees Features Importance', fontweight ="bold",fontsize=14)

    plot1.set_xlabel('Features Importance',  fontsize=10)
    plot1.set_ylabel('Feature Labels',  fontsize=10)
    # Set font for tick labels
    plot1.tick_params(axis='both', which='major', labelsize=5)
    plot1.tick_params(axis='both', which='minor', labelsize=5)
    figure.tight_layout()
    canvas.draw()

def plot_rfe_importance(self, X, y, figure, canvas):
    result_lg = self.obj_data.feat_importance_rfe(X, y)
    figure.clear()
    plot1 = figure.add_subplot(1,1,1)
    sns.set_color_codes("pastel")
    ax=sns.barplot(x = 'Ranking',y = 'Features', data=result_lg, color="orange", ax=plot1)
    plot1.set_title('RFE Features Importance', fontweight ="bold",fontsize=14)

    plot1.set_xlabel('Features Importance',  fontsize=10)
    plot1.set_ylabel('Feature Labels',  fontsize=10)
    # Set font for tick labels
    plot1.tick_params(axis='both', which='major', labelsize=5)
    plot1.tick_params(axis='both', which='minor', labelsize=5)
    figure.tight_layout()
    canvas.draw()

def choose_plot_more(self, df, chosen, X, y, figure1, canvas1, figure2, canvas2):
    if chosen == "Correlation Matrix":
        self.plot_corr_mat(df, figure1, canvas1)

    if chosen == "RF Features Importance":
        self.plot_rf_importance(X, y, figure2, canvas2)
```

```python
    if chosen == "ET Features Importance":
        self.plot_et_importance(X, y, figure1, canvas1)

    if chosen == "RFE Features Importance":
        self.plot_rfe_importance(X, y, figure1, canvas1)

def plot_cm_roc(self, model, X_test, y_test, ypred, name, figure, canvas):
    figure.clear()

    #Plots confusion matrix
    plot1 = figure.add_subplot(2,1,1)
    cm = confusion_matrix(y_test, ypred, )
    sns.heatmap(cm, annot=True, linewidth=3, linecolor='red', fmt='g', cmap="Greens", annot_kws={"size": 14},
ax=plot1)
    plot1.set_title('Confusion Matrix' + " of " + name, fontsize=12)
    plot1.set_xlabel('Y predict', fontsize=10)
    plot1.set_ylabel('Y test', fontsize=10)
    plot1.xaxis.set_ticklabels(['Responsive', 'Not Responsive'], fontsize=10)
    plot1.yaxis.set_ticklabels(['Responsive', 'Not Responsive'], fontsize=10)

    #Plots ROC
    plot2 = figure.add_subplot(2,1,2)
    Y_pred_prob = model.predict_proba(X_test)
    Y_pred_prob = Y_pred_prob[:, 1]

    fpr, tpr, thresholds = roc_curve(y_test, Y_pred_prob)
    plot2.plot([0,1],[0,1], color='navy', linestyle='--', linewidth=3)
    plot2.plot(fpr,tpr, color='red', linewidth=3)
    plot2.set_xlabel('False Positive Rate', fontsize=10)
    plot2.set_ylabel('True Positive Rate', fontsize=10)
    plot2.set_title('ROC Curve of ' + name , fontsize=12)
    plot2.grid(True)

    figure.tight_layout()
    canvas.draw()

#Plots true values versus predicted values diagram and learning curve
def plot_real_pred_val_learning_curve(self, model, X_train, y_train, X_test, y_test, ypred, name, figure, canvas):
    figure.clear()

    #Plots true values versus predicted values diagram
    plot1 = figure.add_subplot(2,1,1)
    acc=accuracy_score(y_test, ypred)
    plot1.scatter(range(len(ypred)),ypred,color="blue", lw=3,label="Predicted")
    plot1.scatter(range(len(y_test)),
        y_test,color="red",label="Actual")
    plot1.set_title("Predicted Values vs True Values of " + name, fontsize=12)
    plot1.set_xlabel("Accuracy: " + str(round((acc*100),3)) + "%")
    plot1.legend()
    plot1.grid(True, alpha=0.75, lw=1, ls='-.')

    #Plots learning curve
    train_sizes=np.linspace(.1, 1.0, 5)
    train_sizes, train_scores, test_scores, fit_times, _ = learning_curve(model,
        X_train, y_train, cv=None, n_jobs=None, train_sizes=train_sizes, return_times=True)
```

```
train_scores_mean = np.mean(train_scores, axis=1)
train_scores_std = np.std(train_scores, axis=1)
test_scores_mean = np.mean(test_scores, axis=1)
test_scores_std = np.std(test_scores, axis=1)

plot2 = figure.add_subplot(2,1,2)
plot2.fill_between(train_sizes, train_scores_mean - train_scores_std,
    train_scores_mean + train_scores_std, alpha=0.1, color="r")
plot2.fill_between(train_sizes, test_scores_mean - test_scores_std,
    test_scores_mean + test_scores_std, alpha=0.1, color="g")
plot2.plot(train_sizes, train_scores_mean, 'o-',
    color="r", label="Training score")
plot2.plot(train_sizes, test_scores_mean, 'o-',
    color="g", label="Cross-validation score")
plot2.legend(loc="best")
plot2.set_title("Learning curve of " + name, fontsize=12)
plot2.set_xlabel("fit_times")
plot2.set_ylabel("Score")
plot2.grid(True, alpha=0.75, lw=1, ls='-.')

figure.tight_layout()
canvas.draw()

def choose_plot_ML(self, root, chosen, X_train, X_test, y_train, y_test, figure1, canvas1, figure2, canvas2):
    if chosen == "Logistic Regression":
        best_model, y_pred = self.obj_ml.implement_LR(chosen, X_train, X_test, y_train, y_test)

        #Plots confusion matrix and ROC
        self.plot_cm_roc(best_model, X_test, y_test, y_pred, chosen, figure1, canvas1)

        #Plots true values versus predicted values diagram and learning curve
        self.plot_real_pred_val_learning_curve(best_model, X_train, y_train,
            X_test, y_test, y_pred, chosen, figure2, canvas2)

        #Shows table of result
        df_lr = self.obj_data.read_dataset("results_LR.csv")
        self.shows_table(root, df_lr, 450, 750, "Y_test and Y_pred of Logistic Regression")

    if chosen == "Random Forest":
        best_model, y_pred = self.obj_ml.implement_RF(chosen, X_train, X_test, y_train, y_test)

        #Plots confusion matrix and ROC
        self.plot_cm_roc(best_model, X_test, y_test, y_pred, chosen, figure1, canvas1)

        #Plots true values versus predicted values diagram and learning curve
        self.plot_real_pred_val_learning_curve(best_model, X_train, y_train,
            X_test, y_test, y_pred, chosen, figure2, canvas2)

        #Shows table of result
        df_lr = self.obj_data.read_dataset("results_RF.csv")
        self.shows_table(root, df_lr, 450, 750, "Y_test and Y_pred of Random Forest")

    if chosen == "K-Nearest Neighbors":
        best_model, y_pred = self.obj_ml.implement_KNN(chosen, X_train, X_test, y_train, y_test)

        #Plots confusion matrix and ROC
```

```
        self.plot_cm_roc(best_model, X_test, y_test, y_pred, chosen, figure1, canvas1)

        #Plots true values versus predicted values diagram and learning curve
        self.plot_real_pred_val_learning_curve(best_model, X_train, y_train,
            X_test, y_test, y_pred, chosen, figure2, canvas2)

        #Shows table of result
        df_lr = self.obj_data.read_dataset("results_KNN.csv")
        self.shows_table(root, df_lr, 450, 750, "Y_test and Y_pred of KNN")

    if chosen == "Decision Trees":
        best_model, y_pred = self.obj_ml.implement_DT(chosen, X_train, X_test, y_train, y_test)

        #Plots confusion matrix and ROC
        self.plot_cm_roc(best_model, X_test, y_test, y_pred, chosen, figure1, canvas1)

        #Plots true values versus predicted values diagram and learning curve
        self.plot_real_pred_val_learning_curve(best_model, X_train, y_train,
            X_test, y_test, y_pred, chosen, figure2, canvas2)

        #Shows table of result
        df_lr = self.obj_data.read_dataset("results_DT.csv")
        self.shows_table(root, df_lr, 450, 750, "Y_test and Y_pred of Decision Trees")

    if chosen == "Gradient Boosting":
        best_model, y_pred = self.obj_ml.implement_GB(chosen, X_train, X_test, y_train, y_test)

        #Plots confusion matrix and ROC
        self.plot_cm_roc(best_model, X_test, y_test, y_pred, chosen, figure1, canvas1)

        #Plots true values versus predicted values diagram and learning curve
        self.plot_real_pred_val_learning_curve(best_model, X_train, y_train,
            X_test, y_test, y_pred, chosen, figure2, canvas2)

        #Shows table of result
        df_lr = self.obj_data.read_dataset("results_GB.csv")
        self.shows_table(root, df_lr, 450, 750, "Y_test and Y_pred of Gradient Boosting")

    if chosen == "Extreme Gradient Boosting":
        best_model, y_pred = self.obj_ml.implement_XGB(chosen, X_train, X_test, y_train, y_test)

        #Plots confusion matrix and ROC
        self.plot_cm_roc(best_model, X_test, y_test, y_pred, chosen, figure1, canvas1)

        #Plots true values versus predicted values diagram and learning curve
        self.plot_real_pred_val_learning_curve(best_model, X_train, y_train,
            X_test, y_test, y_pred, chosen, figure2, canvas2)

        #Shows table of result
        df_lr = self.obj_data.read_dataset("results_XGB.csv")
        self.shows_table(root, df_lr, 450, 750, "Y_test and Y_pred of Extreme Gradient Boosting")

    if chosen == "Multi-Layer Perceptron":
        best_model, y_pred = self.obj_ml.implement_MLP(chosen, X_train, X_test, y_train, y_test)

        #Plots confusion matrix and ROC
```

```
        self.plot_cm_roc(best_model, X_test, y_test, y_pred, chosen, figure1, canvas1)

        #Plots true values versus predicted values diagram and learning curve
        self.plot_real_pred_val_learning_curve(best_model, X_train, y_train,
            X_test, y_test, y_pred, chosen, figure2, canvas2)

        #Shows table of result
        df_lr = self.obj_data.read_dataset("results_MLP.csv")
        self.shows_table(root, df_lr, 450, 750, "Y_test and Y_pred of Multi-Layer Perceptron")

    if chosen == "Support Vector Classifier":
        best_model, y_pred = self.obj_ml.implement_SVC(chosen, X_train, X_test, y_train, y_test)

        #Plots confusion matrix and ROC
        self.plot_cm_roc(best_model, X_test, y_test, y_pred, chosen, figure1, canvas1)

        #Plots true values versus predicted values diagram and learning curve
        self.plot_real_pred_val_learning_curve(best_model, X_train, y_train,
            X_test, y_test, y_pred, chosen, figure2, canvas2)

        #Shows table of result
        df_lr = self.obj_data.read_dataset("results_SVC.csv")
        self.shows_table(root, df_lr, 450, 750, "Y_test and Y_pred of Support Vector Classifier")

    if chosen == "AdaBoost":
        best_model, y_pred = self.obj_ml.implement_ADA(chosen, X_train, X_test, y_train, y_test)

        #Plots confusion matrix and ROC
        self.plot_cm_roc(best_model, X_test, y_test, y_pred, chosen, figure1, canvas1)

        #Plots true values versus predicted values diagram and learning curve
        self.plot_real_pred_val_learning_curve(best_model, X_train, y_train,
            X_test, y_test, y_pred, chosen, figure2, canvas2)

        #Shows table of result
        df_lr = self.obj_data.read_dataset("results_ADA.csv")
        self.shows_table(root, df_lr, 450, 750, "Y_test and Y_pred of AdaBoost Classifier")


def plot_accuracy(self, history, name, figure, canvas):
    acc = history['accuracy']
    val_acc = history['val_accuracy']
    epochs = range(1, len(acc) + 1)

    #Cleans and Creates figure
    figure.clear()
    plot1 = figure.add_subplot(1,1,1)

    # Plots training accuracy in red and validation accuracy in blue dashed line
    plot1.plot(epochs, acc, 'r', label='Training accuracy', lw=3)
    plot1.plot(epochs, val_acc, 'b--', label='Validation accuracy', lw=3)

    # Set plot title and legend
    plot1.set_title('Training and validation accuracy of ' + name, fontsize=12)
    plot1.legend(fontsize=8)
```

```python
        # Set x-axis label and tick label font size
        plot1.set_xlabel("Epoch", fontsize=10)
        plot1.tick_params(labelsize=8)

        # Set background color
        plot1.gca().set_facecolor('black')

        figure.tight_layout()
        canvas.draw()

    def plot_loss(self, history, name, figure, canvas):
        loss = history['loss']
        val_loss = history['val_loss']
        epochs = range(1, len(loss) + 1)

        #Cleans and Creates figure
        figure.clear()
        plot1 = figure.add_subplot(1,1,1)

        # Plot training loss in red and validation loss in blue dashed line
        plot1.plot(epochs, loss, 'r', label='Training loss', lw=3)
        plot1.plot(epochs, val_loss, 'b--', label='Validation loss', lw=3)

        # Set plot title and legend
        plot1.set_title('Training and validation loss of ' + name, fontsize=12)
        plot1.legend(fontsize=8)

        # Set x-axis label and tick label font size
        plot1.set_xlabel("Epoch", fontsize=10)
        plot1.tick_params(labelsize=8)

        # Set background color
        plot1.gca().set_facecolor('lightgray')

        figure.tight_layout()
        canvas.draw()


#process_data.py
import os
import numpy as np
import pandas as pd
from sklearn.preprocessing import LabelEncoder
from sklearn.ensemble import RandomForestClassifier, ExtraTreesClassifier
from sklearn.linear_model import LogisticRegression
from sklearn.feature_selection import RFE

class Process_Data:
    def read_dataset(self, filename):
        #Reads dataset
        curr_path = os.getcwd()
        path = os.path.join(curr_path, filename)
        df = pd.read_csv(path)

        return df

    def preprocess(self):
```

```
df = self.read_dataset("marketing_data.csv")

#Drops ID column
df = df.drop("ID", axis = 1)

#Renames column name and corrects data type
df.rename(columns={' Income ':'Income'},inplace=True)
df["Dt_Customer"] = pd.to_datetime(df["Dt_Customer"], format='%m/%d/%y')
df["Income"] = df["Income"].str.replace("$","").str.replace(",","")
df["Income"] = df["Income"].astype(float)

#Checks null values
print(df.isnull().sum())
print('Total number of null values: ', df.isnull().sum().sum())

#Imputes Income column with median values
df['Income'] = df['Income'].fillna(df['Income'].median())
print(f'Number of Null values in "Income" after Imputation: {df["Income"].isna().sum()}')

#Transformasi Dt_Customer
df['Dt_Customer'] = pd.to_datetime(df['Dt_Customer'])
print(f'After Transformation:\n {df["Dt_Customer"].head()}')
df['Customer_Age'] = df['Dt_Customer'].dt.year - df['Year_Birth']

#Creates number of children/dependents in home by adding 'Kidhome' and 'Teenhome' features
#Creates number of Total_Purchases by adding all the purchases features
#Creates TotalAmount_Spent by adding all the Mnt* features
df['Dt_Customer_Month'] = df['Dt_Customer'].dt.month
df['Dt_Customer_Year'] = df['Dt_Customer'].dt.year
df['Num_Dependants'] = df['Kidhome'] + df['Teenhome']

purchase_features = [c for c in df.columns if 'Purchase' in str(c)]
#Removes 'NumDealsPurchases' from the list above
purchase_features.remove('NumDealsPurchases')
df['Num_TotalPurchases'] = df[purchase_features].sum(axis = 1)

amt_spent_features = [c for c in df.columns if 'Mnt' in str(c)]
df['TotalAmount_Spent'] = df[amt_spent_features].sum(axis = 1)

#Creates a categorical feature using the customer's age by binnning them,
#to help understanding purchasing behaviour
print(f'Min. Customer Age: {df["Customer_Age"].min()}')
print(f'Max. Customer Age: {df["Customer_Age"].max()}')
df['AgeGroup'] = pd.cut(df['Customer_Age'], bins = [6, 24, 29, 40, 56, 75],
    labels = ['Gen-Z', 'Gen-Y.1', 'Gen-Y.2', 'Gen-X', 'BBoomers'])

return df

def categorize(self, df):
    #Creates a dummy dataframe for visualization
    df_dummy=df.copy()

    #Categorizes Income feature
    labels = ['0-20k', '20k-30k', '30k-50k','50k-70k','70k-700k']
    df_dummy['Income'] = pd.cut(df_dummy['Income'],
        [0, 20000, 30000, 50000, 70000, 700000], labels=labels)
```

```
#Categorizes TotalAmount_Spent feature
labels = ['0-200', '200-500', '500-800','800-1000','1000-3000']
df_dummy['TotalAmount_Spent'] = pd.cut(df_dummy['TotalAmount_Spent'],
  [0, 200, 500, 800, 1000, 3000], labels=labels)

#Categorizes Num_TotalPurchases feature
labels = ['0-5', '5-10', '10-15','15-25','25-35']
df_dummy['Num_TotalPurchases'] = pd.cut(df_dummy['Num_TotalPurchases'],
  [0, 5, 10, 15, 25, 35], labels=labels)

#Categorizes Dt_Customer_Year feature
labels = ['2012', '2013', '2014']
df_dummy['Dt_Customer_Year'] = pd.cut(df_dummy['Dt_Customer_Year'],
  [0, 2012, 2013, 2014], labels=labels)

#Categorizes Dt_Customer_Month feature
labels = ['0-3', '3-6', '6-9','9-12']
df_dummy['Dt_Customer_Month'] = pd.cut(df_dummy['Dt_Customer_Month'],
  [0, 3, 6, 9, 12], labels=labels)

#Categorizes Customer_Age feature
labels = ['0-30', '30-40', '40-50', '40-60','60-120']
df_dummy['Customer_Age'] = pd.cut(df_dummy['Customer_Age'],
  [0, 30, 40, 50, 60, 120], labels=labels)

#Categorizes MntGoldProds feature
labels = ['0-30', '30-50', '50-80', '80-100','100-400']
df_dummy['MntGoldProds'] = pd.cut(df_dummy['MntGoldProds'],
  [0, 30, 50, 80, 100, 400], labels=labels)

#Categorizes MntSweetProducts feature
labels = ['0-10', '10-20', '20-40', '40-100','100-300']
df_dummy['MntSweetProducts'] = pd.cut(df_dummy['MntSweetProducts'],
  [0, 10, 20, 40, 100, 300], labels=labels)

#Categorizes MntFishProducts feature
labels = ['0-10', '10-20', '20-40', '40-100','100-300']
df_dummy['MntFishProducts'] = pd.cut(df_dummy['MntFishProducts'],
  [0, 10, 20, 40, 100, 300], labels=labels)

#Categorizes MntMeatProducts feature
labels = ['0-50', '50-100', '100-200', '200-500','500-2000']
df_dummy['MntMeatProducts'] = pd.cut(df_dummy['MntMeatProducts'],
  [0, 50, 100, 200, 500, 2000], labels=labels)

#Categorizes MntFruits feature
labels = ['0-10', '10-30', '30-50', '50-100','100-200']
df_dummy['MntFruits'] = pd.cut(df_dummy['MntFruits'],
  [0, 1, 30, 50, 100, 200], labels=labels)

#Categorizes MntWines feature
labels = ['0-100', '100-300', '300-500', '500-1000','1000-1500']
df_dummy['MntWines'] = pd.cut(df_dummy['MntWines'],
  [0, 100, 300, 500, 1000, 1500], labels=labels)
```

```
#Categorizes Recency feature
labels = ['0-10', '10-30', '30-50', '50-80','80-100']
df_dummy['Recency'] = pd.cut(df_dummy['Recency'],
    [0, 10, 30, 50, 80, 100], labels=labels)

return df_dummy

def extract_cat_num_cols(self, df):
    #Extracts categorical and numerical columns in dummy dataset
    cat_cols = [col for col in df.columns if
        (df[col].dtype == 'object') or (df[col].dtype.name == 'category')]
    num_cols = [col for col in df.columns if
        (df[col].dtype != 'object') and (df[col].dtype.name != 'category')]

    return cat_cols, num_cols

def encode_categorical_feats(self, df, cat_cols):
    #Encodes categorical features in original dataset
    print(f'Features that needs to be Label Encoded: \n{cat_cols}')

    for c in cat_cols:
        lbl = LabelEncoder()
        lbl.fit(list(df[c].astype(str).values))
        df[c] = lbl.transform(list(df[c].astype(str).values))
    print('Label Encoding done..')
    return df

def extract_input_output_vars(self, df):
    #Extracts output and input variables
    y = df['Response'].values # Target for the model
    X = df.drop(['Dt_Customer', 'Year_Birth', 'Response'], axis = 1)

    return X, y

def feat_importance_rf(self, X, y):
    names = X.columns
    rf = RandomForestClassifier()
    rf.fit(X, y)

    result_rf = pd.DataFrame()
    result_rf['Features'] = X.columns
    result_rf ['Values'] = rf.feature_importances_
    result_rf.sort_values('Values', inplace = True, ascending = False)

    return result_rf

def feat_importance_et(self, X, y):
    model = ExtraTreesClassifier()
    model.fit(X, y)

    result_et = pd.DataFrame()
    result_et['Features'] = X.columns
    result_et ['Values'] = model.feature_importances_
    result_et.sort_values('Values', inplace=True, ascending =False)

    return result_et
```

```python
def feat_importance_rfe(self, X, y):
    model = LogisticRegression()
    #Creates the RFE model
    rfe = RFE(model)
    rfe = rfe.fit(X, y)

    result_lg = pd.DataFrame()
    result_lg['Features'] = X.columns
    result_lg ['Ranking'] = rfe.ranking_
    result_lg.sort_values('Ranking', inplace=True , ascending = False)

    return result_lg

def save_result(self, y_test, y_pred, fname):
    # Convert y_test and y_pred to pandas Series for easier handling
    y_test_series = pd.Series(y_test)
    y_pred_series = pd.Series(y_pred)

    # Calculate y_result_series
    y_result_series = pd.Series(y_pred - y_test == 0)
    y_result_series = y_result_series.map({True: 'True', False: 'False'})

    # Create a DataFrame to hold y_test, y_pred, and y_result
    data = pd.DataFrame({'y_test': y_test_series, 'y_pred': y_pred_series, 'result': y_result_series})

    # Save the DataFrame to a CSV file
    data.to_csv(fname, index=False)


#machine_learning.py
import numpy as np
from imblearn.over_sampling import SMOTE
from sklearn.model_selection import train_test_split, RandomizedSearchCV, GridSearchCV, StratifiedKFold
from sklearn.preprocessing import StandardScaler
import joblib
from sklearn.linear_model import LogisticRegression
from sklearn.metrics import confusion_matrix, accuracy_score, recall_score, precision_score
from sklearn.metrics import classification_report, f1_score, plot_confusion_matrix
from sklearn.ensemble import RandomForestClassifier
from sklearn.neighbors import KNeighborsClassifier
from sklearn.tree import DecisionTreeClassifier
from sklearn.ensemble import AdaBoostClassifier, GradientBoostingClassifier
from xgboost import XGBClassifier
from sklearn.neural_network import MLPClassifier
from sklearn.svm import SVC
import os
import joblib
import pandas as pd
from process_data import Process_Data

class Machine_Learning:
    def __init__(self):
        self.obj_data = Process_Data()
```

```python
def oversampling_splitting(self, X, y):
    sm = SMOTE(random_state=42)
    X,y = sm.fit_resample(X, y.ravel())

    #Splits the data into training and testing
    X_train, X_test, y_train, y_test = train_test_split(X, y, test_size = 0.2, random_state = 2021, stratify=y)

    #Use Standard Scaler
    scaler = StandardScaler()
    X_train_stand = scaler.fit_transform(X_train)
    X_test_stand = scaler.transform(X_test)

    #Saves into pkl files
    joblib.dump(X_train_stand, 'X_train.pkl')
    joblib.dump(X_test_stand, 'X_test.pkl')
    joblib.dump(y_train, 'y_train.pkl')
    joblib.dump(y_test, 'y_test.pkl')

def load_files(self):
    X_train = joblib.load('X_train.pkl')
    X_test = joblib.load('X_test.pkl')
    y_train = joblib.load('y_train.pkl')
    y_test = joblib.load('y_test.pkl')

    return X_train, X_test, y_train, y_test

def choose_feats_boundary(self, X, y):
    file_path = os.getcwd()
    X_train_feat_path = os.path.join(file_path, 'X_train_feat.pkl')
    X_test_feat_path = os.path.join(file_path, 'X_test_feat.pkl')
    y_train_feat_path = os.path.join(file_path, 'y_train_feat.pkl')
    y_test_feat_path = os.path.join(file_path, 'y_test_feat.pkl')

    if os.path.exists(X_train_feat_path):
        X_train_feat = joblib.load(X_train_feat_path)
        X_test_feat = joblib.load(X_test_feat_path)
        y_train_feat = joblib.load(y_train_feat_path)
        y_test_feat = joblib.load(y_test_feat_path)
    else:
        # Make sure feat_boundary contains valid column indices from your X array
        feat_boundary = [1, 2]  # actual indices
        if all(idx < X.shape[1] for idx in feat_boundary):
            X_feature = X[:, feat_boundary]
            X_train_feat, X_test_feat, y_train_feat, y_test_feat = train_test_split(X_feature, y,
                test_size=0.2, random_state=2021, stratify=y)

            # Saves into pkl files
            joblib.dump(X_train_feat, X_train_feat_path)
            joblib.dump(X_test_feat, X_test_feat_path)
            joblib.dump(y_train_feat, y_train_feat_path)
            joblib.dump(y_test_feat, y_test_feat_path)
        else:
            raise ValueError("Indices in feat_boundary exceed the number of columns in X array")

    return X_train_feat, X_test_feat, y_train_feat, y_test_feat
```

```python
def train_model(self, model, X, y):
    model.fit(X, y)
    return model

def predict_model(self, model, X, proba=False):
    if ~proba:
        y_pred = model.predict(X)
    else:
        y_pred_proba = model.predict_proba(X)
        y_pred = np.argmax(y_pred_proba, axis=1)

    return y_pred

def run_model(self, name, model, X_train, X_test, y_train, y_test, proba=False):
    y_pred = self.predict_model(model, X_test, proba)

    accuracy = accuracy_score(y_test, y_pred)
    recall = recall_score(y_test, y_pred, average='weighted')
    precision = precision_score(y_test, y_pred, average='weighted')
    f1 = f1_score(y_test, y_pred, average='weighted')

    print(name)
    print('accuracy: ', accuracy)
    print('recall: ', recall)
    print('precision: ', precision)
    print('f1: ', f1)
    print(classification_report(y_test, y_pred))

    return y_pred

def logistic_regression(self, name, X_train, X_test, y_train, y_test):
    #Logistic Regression Classifier
    # Define the parameter grid for the grid search
    param_grid = {
        'C': [0.01, 0.1, 1, 10],
        'penalty': ['none', 'l2'],
        'solver': ['newton-cg', 'lbfgs', 'liblinear', 'saga'],
    }

    # Initialize the Logistic Regression model
    logreg = LogisticRegression(max_iter=5000, random_state=2021)

    # Create GridSearchCV with the Logistic Regression model and the parameter grid
    grid_search = GridSearchCV(logreg, param_grid, cv=3, scoring='accuracy', n_jobs=-1)

    # Train and perform grid search
    grid_search.fit(X_train, y_train)

    # Get the best Logistic Regression model from the grid search
    best_model = grid_search.best_estimator_

    #Saves model
    joblib.dump(best_model, 'LR_Model.pkl')

    # Print the best hyperparameters found
    print(f"Best Hyperparameters for LR:")
```

```python
    print(grid_search.best_params_)

    return best_model

def implement_LR(self, chosen, X_train, X_test, y_train, y_test):
    file_path = os.getcwd()+"/LR_Model.pkl"
    if os.path.exists(file_path):
        model = joblib.load('LR_Model.pkl')
        y_pred = self.run_model(chosen, model, X_train, X_test, y_train, y_test, proba=True)
    else:
        model = self.logistic_regression(chosen, X_train, X_test, y_train, y_test)
        y_pred = self.run_model(chosen, model, X_train, X_test, y_train, y_test, proba=True)

    #Saves result into excel file
    self.obj_data.save_result(y_test, y_pred, "results_LR.csv")

    print("Training Logistic Regression done...")
    return model, y_pred

def random_forest(self, name, X_train, X_test, y_train, y_test):
    #Random Forest Classifier
    # Define the parameter grid for the grid search
    param_grid = {
        'n_estimators': [100, 200, 300],
        'max_depth': [10, 20, 30, 40, 50],
        'min_samples_split': [2, 5, 10],
        'min_samples_leaf': [1, 2, 4]
    }

    # Initialize the RandomForestClassifier model
    rf = RandomForestClassifier(random_state=2021)

    # Create GridSearchCV with the RandomForestClassifier model and the parameter grid
    grid_search = GridSearchCV(rf, param_grid, cv=3, scoring='accuracy', n_jobs=-1)

    # Train and perform grid search
    grid_search.fit(X_train, y_train)

    # Get the best RandomForestClassifier model from the grid search
    best_model = grid_search.best_estimator_

    #Saves model
    joblib.dump(best_model, 'RF_Model.pkl')

    # Print the best hyperparameters found
    print(f"Best Hyperparameters for RF:")
    print(grid_search.best_params_)

    return best_model

def implement_RF(self, chosen, X_train, X_test, y_train, y_test):
    file_path = os.getcwd()+"/RF_Model.pkl"
    if os.path.exists(file_path):
        model = joblib.load('RF_Model.pkl')
        y_pred = self.run_model(chosen, model, X_train, X_test, y_train, y_test, proba=True)
    else:
```

```python
        model = self.random_forest(chosen, X_train, X_test, y_train, y_test)
        y_pred = self.run_model(chosen, model, X_train, X_test, y_train, y_test, proba=True)

        #Saves result into excel file
        self.obj_data.save_result(y_test, y_pred, "results_RF.csv")

        print("Training Random Forest done...")
        return model, y_pred

    def knearest_neigbors(self, name, X_train, X_test, y_train, y_test):
        #KNN Classifier
        # Define the parameter grid for the grid search
        param_grid = {
            'n_neighbors': list(range(2, 10))
        }

        # Initialize the KNN Classifier
        knn = KNeighborsClassifier()

        # Create GridSearchCV with the KNN model and the parameter grid
        grid_search = GridSearchCV(knn, param_grid, cv=3, scoring='accuracy', n_jobs=-1)

        # Train and perform grid search
        grid_search.fit(X_train, y_train)

        # Get the best KNN model from the grid search
        best_model = grid_search.best_estimator_

        #Saves model
        joblib.dump(best_model, 'KNN_Model.pkl')

        # Print the best hyperparameters found
        print(f"Best Hyperparameters for KNN:")
        print(grid_search.best_params_)

        return best_model

    def implement_KNN(self, chosen, X_train, X_test, y_train, y_test):
        file_path = os.getcwd()+"/KNN_Model.pkl"
        if os.path.exists(file_path):
            model = joblib.load('KNN_Model.pkl')
            y_pred = self.run_model(chosen, model, X_train, X_test, y_train, y_test, proba=True)
        else:
            model = self.knearest_neigbors(chosen, X_train, X_test, y_train, y_test)
            y_pred = self.run_model(chosen, model, X_train, X_test, y_train, y_test, proba=True)

        #Saves result into excel file
        self.obj_data.save_result(y_test, y_pred, "results_KNN.csv")

        print("Training KNN done...")
        return model, y_pred

    def decision_trees(self, name, X_train, X_test, y_train, y_test):
        # Initialize the DecisionTreeClassifier model
        dt_clf = DecisionTreeClassifier(random_state=2021)
```

```python
    # Define the parameter grid for the grid search
    param_grid = {
        'max_depth': np.arange(1, 51, 1),
        'criterion': ['gini', 'entropy'],
        'min_samples_split': [2, 5, 10],
        'min_samples_leaf': [1, 2, 4],
    }

    # Create GridSearchCV with the DecisionTreeClassifier model and the parameter grid
    grid_search = GridSearchCV(dt_clf, param_grid, cv=3, scoring='accuracy', n_jobs=-1)

    # Train and perform grid search
    grid_search.fit(X_train, y_train)

    # Get the best DecisionTreeClassifier model from the grid search
    best_model = grid_search.best_estimator_

    #Saves model
    joblib.dump(best_model, 'DT_Model.pkl')

    # Print the best hyperparameters found
    print(f"Best Hyperparameters for DT:")
    print(grid_search.best_params_)

    return best_model

def implement_DT(self, chosen, X_train, X_test, y_train, y_test):
    file_path = os.getcwd()+"/DT_Model.pkl"
    if os.path.exists(file_path):
        model = joblib.load('DT_Model.pkl')
        y_pred = self.run_model(chosen, model, X_train, X_test, y_train, y_test, proba=True)
    else:
        model = self.decision_trees(chosen, X_train, X_test, y_train, y_test)
        y_pred = self.run_model(chosen, model, X_train, X_test, y_train, y_test, proba=True)

    #Saves result into excel file
    self.obj_data.save_result(y_test, y_pred, "results_DT.csv")

    print("Training Decision Trees done...")
    return model, y_pred

def gradient_boosting(self, name, X_train, X_test, y_train, y_test):
    #Gradient Boosting Classifier
    # Initialize the GradientBoostingClassifier model
    gbt = GradientBoostingClassifier(random_state=2021)

    # Define the parameter grid for the grid search
    param_grid = {
        'n_estimators': [100, 200, 300],
        'max_depth': [10, 20, 30],
        'subsample': [0.6, 0.8, 1.0],
        'max_features': [0.2, 0.4, 0.6, 0.8, 1.0],
    }

    # Create GridSearchCV with the GradientBoostingClassifier model and the parameter grid
    grid_search = GridSearchCV(gbt, param_grid, cv=3, scoring='accuracy', n_jobs=-1)
```

```
# Train and perform grid search
grid_search.fit(X_train, y_train)

# Get the best GradientBoostingClassifier model from the grid search
best_model = grid_search.best_estimator_

#Saves model
joblib.dump(best_model, 'GB_Model.pkl')

# Print the best hyperparameters found
print(f"Best Hyperparameters for GB:")
print(grid_search.best_params_)

return best_model

def implement_GB(self, chosen, X_train, X_test, y_train, y_test):
    file_path = os.getcwd()+"/GB_Model.pkl"
    if os.path.exists(file_path):
        model = joblib.load('GB_Model.pkl')
        y_pred = self.run_model(chosen, model, X_train, X_test, y_train, y_test, proba=True)
    else:
        model = self.gradient_boosting(chosen, X_train, X_test, y_train, y_test)
        y_pred = self.run_model(chosen, model, X_train, X_test, y_train, y_test, proba=True)

    #Saves result into excel file
    self.obj_data.save_result(y_test, y_pred, "results_GB.csv")

    print("Training Gradient Boosting done...")
    return model, y_pred

# def light_gradient_boosting(self, name, X_train, X_test, y_train, y_test):
#     #LGBM Classifier
#     # Define the parameter grid for grid search
#     param_grid = {
#         'max_depth': [10, 20, 30],
#         'n_estimators': [100, 200, 300],
#         'subsample': [0.6, 0.8, 1.0],
#         'random_state': [2021]
#     }

#     # Initialize the LightGBM classifier
#     lgbm = LGBMClassifier()

#     # Create GridSearchCV with the LightGBM classifier and the parameter grid
#     grid_search = GridSearchCV(lgbm, param_grid, cv=3, scoring='accuracy', n_jobs=-1)

#     # Train and perform grid search
#     grid_search.fit(X_train, y_train)

#     # Get the best LightGBM classifier model from the grid search
#     best_model = grid_search.best_estimator_

#     #Saves model
#     joblib.dump(best_model, 'LGB_Model.pkl')
```

```
#    # Print the best hyperparameters found
#    print(f"Best Hyperparameters for LGB:")
#    print(grid_search.best_params_)

#    return best_model

# def implement_LGB(self, chosen, X_train, X_test, y_train, y_test):
#    file_path = os.getcwd()+"/LGB_Model.pkl"
#    if os.path.exists(file_path):
#        model = joblib.load('LGB_Model.pkl')
#        y_pred = self.run_model(chosen, model, X_train, X_test, y_train, y_test, proba=True)
#    else:
#        model = self.light_gradient_boosting(chosen, X_train, X_test, y_train, y_test)
#        y_pred = self.run_model(chosen, model, X_train, X_test, y_train, y_test, proba=True)

#    #Saves result into excel file
#    self.save_result(y_test, y_pred, "results_LGB.csv")

#    print("Training Light Gradient Boosting done...")
#    return model, y_pred

def extreme_gradient_boosting(self, name, X_train, X_test, y_train, y_test):
    # Define the parameter grid for the grid search
    param_grid = {
        'n_estimators': [100, 200, 300],
        'max_depth': [10, 20, 30],
        'learning_rate': [0.01, 0.1, 0.2],
        'subsample': [0.6, 0.8, 1.0],
        'colsample_bytree': [0.6, 0.8, 1.0],
    }

    # Initialize the XGBoost classifier
    xgb = XGBClassifier(random_state=2021, use_label_encoder=False, eval_metric='mlogloss')

    # Create GridSearchCV with the XGBoost classifier and the parameter grid
    grid_search = GridSearchCV(xgb, param_grid, cv=3, scoring='accuracy', n_jobs=-1)

    # Train and perform grid search
    grid_search.fit(X_train, y_train)

    # Get the best XGBoost classifier model from the grid search
    best_model = grid_search.best_estimator_

    #Saves model
    joblib.dump(best_model, 'XGB_Model.pkl')

    # Print the best hyperparameters found
    print(f"Best Hyperparameters for XGB:")
    print(grid_search.best_params_)

    return best_model

def implement_XGB(self, chosen, X_train, X_test, y_train, y_test):
    file_path = os.getcwd()+"/XGB_Model.pkl"
    if os.path.exists(file_path):
        model = joblib.load('XGB_Model.pkl')
```

```python
            y_pred = self.run_model(chosen, model, X_train, X_test, y_train, y_test, proba=True)
        else:
            model = self.extreme_gradient_boosting(chosen, X_train, X_test, y_train, y_test)
            y_pred = self.run_model(chosen, model, X_train, X_test, y_train, y_test, proba=True)

        #Saves result into excel file
        self.obj_data.save_result(y_test, y_pred, "results_XGB.csv")

        print("Training Extreme Gradient Boosting done...")
        return model, y_pred

    def multi_layer_perceptron(self, name, X_train, X_test, y_train, y_test):
        # Define the parameter grid for the grid search
        param_grid = {
            'hidden_layer_sizes': [(50,), (100,), (50, 50), (100, 50), (100, 100)],
            'activation': ['logistic', 'relu'],
            'solver': ['adam', 'sgd'],
            'alpha': [0.0001, 0.001, 0.01],
            'learning_rate': ['constant', 'invscaling', 'adaptive'],
        }

        # Initialize the MLP Classifier
        mlp = MLPClassifier(random_state=2021)

        # Create GridSearchCV with the MLP Classifier and the parameter grid
        grid_search = GridSearchCV(mlp, param_grid, cv=3, scoring='accuracy', n_jobs=-1)

        # Train and perform grid search
        grid_search.fit(X_train, y_train)

        # Get the best MLP Classifier model from the grid search
        best_model = grid_search.best_estimator_

        #Saves model
        joblib.dump(best_model, 'MLP_Model.pkl')

        # Print the best hyperparameters found
        print(f"Best Hyperparameters for MLP:")
        print(grid_search.best_params_)

        return best_model

    def implement_MLP(self, chosen, X_train, X_test, y_train, y_test):
        file_path = os.getcwd()+"/MLP_Model.pkl"
        if os.path.exists(file_path):
            model = joblib.load('MLP_Model.pkl')
            y_pred = self.run_model(chosen, model, X_train, X_test, y_train, y_test, proba=True)
        else:
            model = self.multi_layer_perceptron(chosen, X_train, X_test, y_train, y_test)
            y_pred = self.run_model(chosen, model, X_train, X_test, y_train, y_test, proba=True)

        #Saves result into excel file
        self.obj_data.save_result(y_test, y_pred, "results_MLP.csv")

        print("Training Multi-Layer Perceptron done...")
        return model, y_pred
```

```python
def support_vector(self, name, X_train, X_test, y_train, y_test):
    #Support Vector Classifier
    # Define the parameter grid for the grid search
    param_grid = {
        'C': [0.1, 1, 10],
        'kernel': ['linear', 'poly', 'rbf'],
        'gamma': ['scale', 'auto', 0.1, 1],
    }

    # Initialize the SVC model
    model_svc = SVC(random_state=2021, probability=True)

    # Create GridSearchCV with the SVC model and the parameter grid
    grid_search = GridSearchCV(model_svc, param_grid, cv=3, scoring='accuracy', n_jobs=-1, refit=True)

    # Train and perform grid search
    grid_search.fit(X_train, y_train)

    # Get the best MLP Classifier model from the grid search
    best_model = grid_search.best_estimator_

    #Saves model
    joblib.dump(best_model, 'SVC_Model.pkl')

    # Print the best hyperparameters found
    print(f"Best Hyperparameters for SVC:")
    print(grid_search.best_params_)

    return best_model

def implement_SVC(self, chosen, X_train, X_test, y_train, y_test):
    file_path = os.getcwd()+"/SVC_Model.pkl"
    if os.path.exists(file_path):
        model = joblib.load('SVC_Model.pkl')
        y_pred = self.run_model(chosen, model, X_train, X_test, y_train, y_test, proba=True)
    else:
        model = self.support_vector(chosen, X_train, X_test, y_train, y_test)
        y_pred = self.run_model(chosen, model, X_train, X_test, y_train, y_test, proba=True)

    #Saves result into excel file
    self.obj_data.save_result(y_test, y_pred, "results_SVC.csv")

    print("Training Support Vector Classifier done...")
    return model, y_pred

def adaboost_classifier(self, name, X_train, X_test, y_train, y_test):
    # Define the parameter grid for the grid search
    param_grid = {
        'n_estimators': [50, 100, 150],
        'learning_rate': [0.01, 0.1, 0.2],
    }

    # Initialize the AdaBoost classifier
    adaboost = AdaBoostClassifier(random_state=2021)
```

```
# Create GridSearchCV with the AdaBoost classifier and the parameter grid
grid_search = GridSearchCV(adaboost, param_grid, cv=3, scoring='accuracy', n_jobs=-1)

# Train and perform grid search
grid_search.fit(X_train, y_train)

# Get the best AdaBoost Classifier model from the grid search
best_model = grid_search.best_estimator_

#Saves model
joblib.dump(best_model, 'ADA_Model.pkl')

# Print the best hyperparameters found
print(f"Best Hyperparameters for AdaBoost:")
print(grid_search.best_params_)

return best_model

def implement_ADA(self, chosen, X_train, X_test, y_train, y_test):
    file_path = os.getcwd()+"/ADA_Model.pkl"
    if os.path.exists(file_path):
        model = joblib.load('ADA_Model.pkl')
        y_pred = self.run_model(chosen, model, X_train, X_test, y_train, y_test, proba=True)
    else:
        model = self.adaboost_classifier(chosen, X_train, X_test, y_train, y_test)
        y_pred = self.run_model(chosen, model, X_train, X_test, y_train, y_test, proba=True)

    #Saves result into excel file
    self.obj_data.save_result(y_test, y_pred, "results_ADA.csv")

    print("Training AdaBoost done...")
    return model, y_pred
```

Bibliography

Vivian Siahaan and Rismon Hasiholan Sianipar. *STEP BY STEP TUTORIAL: SQL SERVER FOR DATA SCIENCE WITH PYTHON GUI*. North Sumatera: Balige Publishing, 2022.

Vivian Siahaan and Rismon Hasiholan Sianipar. *FULL SOURCE CODE: SQL SERVER FOR STUDENTS AND DATA SCIENTISTS WITH PYTHON GUI*. North Sumatera: Balige Publishing, 2022.

Vivian Siahaan and Rismon Hasiholan Sianipar. *Practical Data Science Programming for Medical Datasets Analysis and Prediction with Python GUI*. North Sumatera: Balige Publishing, 2021.

Vivian Siahaan and Rismon Hasiholan Sianipar. *TEXT PROCESSING AND SENTIMENT ANALYSIS USING MACHINE LEARNING AND DEEP LEARNING WITH PYTHON GUI*. North Sumatera: Balige Publishing, 2022.

Vivian Siahaan and Rismon Hasiholan Sianipar. *RFM ANALYSIS AND K-MEANS CLUSTERING: A CASE STUDY ANALYSIS, CLUSTERING, AND PREDICTION ON RETAIL STORE TRANSACTIONS WITH PYTHON GUI.* North Sumatera: Balige Publishing, 2022.

Vivian Siahaan and Rismon Hasiholan Sianipar. *ONLINE RETAIL CLUSTERING AND PREDICTION USING MACHINE LEARNING WITH PYTHON GUI.* North Sumatera: Balige Publishing, 2022.